MANCHESTER UNITED

74/75

THE PLAYERS' STORIES

By Wayne Barton and Tommy Docherty
With Martin Buchan, Sammy McIlroy, Lou Macari,
Arnie Sidebottom and Brian Greenhoff

EMPIRE
PUBLICATIONS

First published in 2015

EMPIRE PUBLICATIONS
1 Newton Street, Manchester M1 1HW
© Wayne Barton 2015

ISBN: 9781909360334
Cover by DRDSTUDIO

CONTENTS

Dedicated to Brian Greenhoff

ACKNOWLEDGEMENTS

I WISH TO THANK the following people for their help and assistance in this project. Firstly, of course, Brian Greenhoff, to whom this book is dedicated. To Tommy Docherty - it is truly an honour and a privilege to say I worked with him. Sammy McIlroy, who spoke of this season with such enthusiasm, and Lou Macari and Gordon Hill. Very special thanks to Martin Buchan who could not have been more of a help.

Also many thanks to Dan Burdett whose help and enthusiasm for this book has been crucial. Huge thanks to Dan Rose for the cover design and Ash and all at Empire. Thanks to Roy Cavanagh for his assistance. Thanks to my wife, my mum and all my family for their support.

INTRODUCTION

THERE ARE MANY SEASONS, many glorious seasons, in the history of Manchester United and so many words have been written about the triumphs of 1968, 1999 and 2008. The reigns of Sir Matt Busby and Sir Alex Ferguson. The careers of the likes of Sir Bobby Charlton and George Best.

So why a record of the 1974/75 season which, to all intents and purposes, should be acknowledged as the post-war low point for the club? Well, besides the obvious point that 2015 represents forty years since that season, it could be argued that, in fact, it was in 1975 when the modern Manchester United and all it became thereafter was born.

The idea for putting it all together came about over a conversation with Brian Greenhoff in his local pub, the Horse and Farrier in Rochdale, in February 2013. His would be the narrative voice, setting the scene with his remarkable memory of games and events. Through conversation with his former team-mates and manager, the story would fall into place and be told in the most authentic manner. Their story in their words.

Then, tragically, before we'd even had a chance to begin, Brian died in May 2013. Plans to write this book were shelved. The idea remained, and, recalling Brian's passion for the idea, and after conversations with his sons, I decided to write it in his honour, remaining as faithful to the original vision as possible.

Using recordings from our work together on his 2012 autobiography, Brian's memories of that season are included. Lou Macari, Sammy McIlroy, Martin Buchan and the manager, Tommy

Docherty all agreed to be interviewed for this book without any hesitation whatsoever and, in fact, Tommy was so forthcoming once he knew the origins of the idea that he went above and beyond what I had asked. His assistance was so profound that I was honoured and humbled. I hadn't expected Martin Buchan to even respond, even though I knew that in order for the record to be as complete as Brian and I wanted it to be, he needed to be included. I was star struck for most of the hour and a half he gave me.

Some people claim 'the Doc' is unpredictable and that may well be true but you can only take people as you find them and to me, he has been nothing less than a perfect gentleman. He invited me to his home twice to do the forewords for the autobiographies of Brian Greenhoff and Gordon Hill, and demonstrated just as much enthusiasm for this project.

In the mid 1970's Docherty was quoted in a short 'fun' Q&S with *Shoot!* magazine as saying that if he were not a football manager, he'd be a stand-up comedian. In later years, he made his living as an after dinner speaker, and anyone fortunate enough to spend time with him is often treated to some of that tried and tested routine. Tommy has led such an intriguing and fascinating life that sometimes some areas haven't been documented as well as others and it was my intention to penetrate the bravado when asking him his thoughts on the 1974/75 season and the immediate events beforehand. I wanted to go deeper than the anecdotes and find more about the confidence of the man who went from feeling vulnerable in his position to then being so confident that he implemented an nfrastructure that would form the foundations on which later success was built. He didn't disappoint.

What became clear from talking to him was that while wingers were an important part of his formation, the attitude of his team was far more important. This book studies the evolution of that formation and philosophy as it began to take shape, as well as last minute defeat to a star-studded Brazil team – we did ourselves justice because we had a great side. Craig Brown later gave me a great compliment by saying that statistically I had the best win record of any permanent Scotland manager and of course, as a fiercely proud Scot, that was very pleasing.

However, just as I'd missed British football, now I was beginning to miss the daily plan of club football. I missed the activity, a game every week, training every day. I went to see Crystal Palace beat Manchester United 5-0 at Selhurst Park in December 1972. One of my striking memories that day was popping in the changing rooms during the game and seeing Denis Law, who had been named as a substitute, still in there – notorious for disliking watching games when he wanted to be playing (as he still is to this day), Denis refused to sit on the bench.

Sir Matt Busby, God rest his soul, did watch that game and seemingly decided that was the point he'd had enough of Frank O'Farrell. It was almost like history repeating itself for me as Sir Matt asked how I would like the United job. "But you've got a manager," I queried. "We won't have one on Wednesday," Sir Matt responded.

The first thing I did was approach Frank, as not only had we played together, but he was also Godfather to one of my sons.

"Frank, I've just been spoken to by Sir Matt, Louis Edwards, and Les Olive. They've offered me your job at Old Trafford," I said, cautiously.

"Oh don't be bothered by that," was his reply.

"What should I do?"

"Take it!" Frank replied, "If you don't take it, someone else will... I'd rather you did than someone else."

In April 1974, following relegation from Division One, Sir Matt called me for a meeting which I felt would be the opposite of the one we'd had at Selhurst - I felt there was a fair chance of me getting the sack. Instead, he gave me a case of champagne.

I was disappointed of course. Not with the champagne, but the relegation. I felt I could have done better. I knew the players I'd taken on when I accepted the job. Bobby Charlton, Denis Law, George Best. I was upset with myself that I had taken Manchester United down and the spotlight was burning even brighter than usual because a number of great players had come to the end and even though I had to move them on, I was still questioned for doing so. Only Denis was really my call – Bobby came to see me and asked if it was okay to retire. I was always thankful for Bobby for that, it was very nice. And George, of course, well that is already well documented...

I was trying to build a team together and felt that we were getting there towards the end of the 1973/74 season but it was just too late. Lou Macari had struggled to live up to the weight of expectation in his early days and Sammy McIlroy had suffered with a huge dip in confidence after his car crash, as much as I tried to keep faith and see him come good. The natural anxiety to impress as young players in a struggling side may well have been a contributing factor towards our relegation – not that it was their fault in the slightest. I may have held on to one or two of the older players for too long but I knew that in Lou and Sammy that they would come good.

From then on, the club had put their faith in me too, but it could be fair to say it was a gamble on their part and then every major decision I was making was a gamble as well.

After a relegation there is a tendency for teams to make a number of changes but I had been convinced that we were on the right path. You can never say for certain but if the season had lasted a month longer, or had we got into form a month earlier, then it could have all been a different story. I'd like to think we could have stayed up. But it's a case of *que sera sera*, like so many other things. Either way, I was confident that continuity and consistency with the majority of players we had would be the best thing. I still felt we needed one or two. As I say, in a perfect world, Manchester United would have been in the top flight contending for top names and it is self explanatory that if you buy a top player you are bringing proven, established talent to the club. I was always fond of finding a player with potential and giving him a chance – and this was the case with Stuart Pearson. I had seen Stuart in my time at Hull, playing alongside Ken Wagstaff, and I thought he had great potential. Quick, sharp, alert, a nice lad and a great trainer. Hull had two established strikers and 'Pancho' as he was known would only get a game if one was injured. I made an offer of £100,000 and one of our youth players.

People had probably never heard of Stuart and with it being a large fee, Brian Kidd having gone, and United being in Division Two, perhaps they thought it was a risk, but I knew exactly what I was getting with him. It was just a matter of giving him an opportunity. Attracting players to Manchester United was never a problem, even then. Everybody wanted to come, nobody wanted to leave. But you must take into consideration that a match day squad was the starting eleven and one substitute – players always want to be involved and it was a lot harder to justify having a squad that had too many players for that reason.

I would have liked to have gotten a goalkeeper in even at this stage. Alex Stepney had been a great keeper for United but I felt the time was right to replace him. Attempts to sign Gordon Banks, and later, Peter Shilton, didn't come to fruition. I did sign Paddy Roche, but that move was a disaster to say the least. The turnover of players in the run up to relegation had been hit and miss. Stewart Houston was a great defender but Mick Martin didn't work out as well as I would have hoped; Gerry Daly was a fine midfielder, a terrific player even if he liked too much of a good time, and I had hoped George Graham would replicate the form he'd had under me at Chelsea, but he was following Bobby Charlton and it was just too much for him.

There was some positivity towards the end of the '73/74 season but relegation came as a body blow and was bitterly disappointing. I was therefore naturally very happy to see the players immediately adapt to their new surroundings in the Second Division and establish a lead very early on in the '74/75 campaign. Winning can become a habit and success breeds success and we just felt that we could attack for ninety minutes. Sometimes, that's what it felt like I was watching. A couple of years later we played Spurs at White Hart Lane and played them off the pitch. Bill Nicholson tapped me on the shoulder and said, "Well done Tom, great win. You've a good side who are great to watch... what I like about you is that you can't tell if you're winning 5-0 or losing 5-0." A young Glenn Hoddle chipped in and said, "Not very good defending though," and Nicholson snapped at him and said "How do you know, you never see them defending!" That attitude was something that was developed in those days in the Second Division when the formation of that team was coming together.

Behind the scenes things were coming together too. Frank Blunstone turned down a move to become Chelsea manager early in the season and this pleased me greatly – he was a fantastic developer of talent, wonderful as a worker with young players of 17 or 18. He was a great judge of young talent, very much in the mould of Jimmy Murphy, who was another I never felt got the credit he quite deserved for the work he did in rebuilding the club after the Munich Air Disaster. Frank was a great youth coach but I don't think he was suited to be a manager and the same could be said of Tommy Cavanagh. A great number two, but never a number one in a million years, and although he wasn't technically my assistant at this time, he performed all the duties of that role.

He would hate flash – he detested backheels for example. "Nine out of ten don't come off," I can still remember him saying. He was a hard taskmaster but deep down the players loved him, of that I'm sure.

I used to love a Friday afternoon after training, going out to Mottram Hall and having a bit of dinner, just chilling out and preparing for the next day... I really couldn't wait for the Saturday. I couldn't wait to see my team play. They were great to watch. Not just as a manager but as a spectator and a supporter too. I'd rub my hands together and say, "Roll on Saturday!" It really was a marvellous time.

The good start we had made had played a part in the positive mood. I may have had concerns about whether or not I would be deemed suitable to continue the job in the eyes of others but I was always confident in my own ability to take United back and set things right. I never wavered on that front. I knew you have your good times and bad times in football.

And of course, we did have a bad time, as all teams do. There are always a number of reasons why. I would not put it down to complacency, though. There was no chance of that. Playing in Division Two meant that these Manchester United players had a lot to prove. There was no danger of them getting too big for their boots, even if that was a danger that might follow a year or so later. What the players had got was some vindication in their self-belief that they were as good as they appeared to be when they took on and beat some top First Division sides in the League Cup. Playing with better players makes you better, as does playing against better opponents. It makes you a better team. And although, looking back on it, there were times during the '74/75 season when it seemed as if the League Cup was more of a nuisance, I was disappointed to go out, as I was disappointed to go out at any stage of a Cup competition or lose any game of football.

I still felt there was progress there. You can't always say defeat is bad as it helps players focus and correct things that weren't quite there in their games. Simply put, it's experience. The experience of relegation had put a weight on their shoulders... we collectively accepted the responsibility and were all the better for it. The Cup disappointment was a good learning ground for later on.

The Norwich game saw a low point in our season in more ways than one as our travelling support once again made the headlines for bad behaviour in and around the ground. Looking back through this record I remember a fair few attempts to try and calm it down. But in hindsight, you have to remember that we were sometimes taking more supporters to away games than the home team had. I remember the first game of the season and seeing our supporters getting thrown out of the ground at Leyton Orient - I gave a few of them complimentary tickets to get back in!

Our patchy form for that short spell in the late winter could be down to a number of reasons. The return game against Orient saw them employ tactics I described as 'pathetic' at the time. In fairness, in those days, I will admit I said a lot of things that were out of order, and a fair few of those things are recalled here. Sometimes I look back and see things I've said and think, "Surely I didn't say that!" but it's all documented and I can't argue with it... some words were out of order and stupid. You get more experienced and deal with things better, so you don't always react with such comments in the heat of the moment, even though other managers might try and wind you up.

One name you might expect would do that was Brian Clough, who I came up against in March after he'd just taken over at Nottingham Forest. But I'd always got on well with Brian, even when he'd been at Derby County. He was brilliant. Win, draw or lose - as he did on this particular day - he was always fabulously welcoming after a game with a bottle of champagne. Brian was still recovering from his time at Leeds, a period on which the film 'The Damned United' was based. The same could have been said for our United in the early days of this season, though I was grateful for the backing of my board which of course Brian did not enjoy at Derby. Brian never got on with his chairman at Derby but he ran the show there – when he arrived at Leeds, he took the players down a peg or two right away. I suppose some people might have found it odd to see Brian and I pitting our wits against each other in the Second Division but it was a sign of the competitiveness of the time.

Like Cloughie, I said what I thought – and that's what I did at the time, as proved by my comments about the Orient game, or after our bruising encounters with Hull City. I was learning. Still, I did think the approach from our opponents was sometimes too much. Some people thought we were great to watch but if they roughed us up they'd get a better chance of getting a result. Our players tried to match that but it just wasn't within them. When you are players of flair you can't change your game. What you can do is be robust and toughen up in yourself. They were learning too.

There was an obvious concern when things are going wrong that they might stay that way but what you have to do is get back to basics. Everyone hits bad patches and what we had to do was reset and remind ourselves what we were good at. Good passing. Fast movement. Less reliance on crossing. We didn't cross high because our forwards were five foot eight. Cav used to drum it in to them in training. "VIOLENCE!" he would bellow, wanting the wingers to smash the crosses in and pulverise the ball. Macari and Pearson were both so great at taking balls in that manner.

Going back to basics meant being a bit more focused and responsible. We had led the table for such a long time and promotion seemed a certainty but I wanted to ensure that rather than slip away – as we saw happen to Sunderland.

I used to get phone calls from clubs and pubs telling me such and such player was in. We had a rule book saying that players couldn't go out drinking from Thursday nights. One Thursday night I got a phone call just after 6pm. "Mr Docherty, Pearson's just come in, with Macari, and Jimmy McCalliog," said the voice. I went down to the pub and they were all stood at the bar having a great time. "Hello gaffer, how are ya," they welcomed me.

"What's your drink?"

"A gin and tonic," I answer. I have the drink and get up to leave.

"Thanks for the drinks lads," I say. "By the way, here's a letter for each of you, read it in the morning."

I fined them two weeks wages.

The players began to respond positively. I mentioned Sammy McIlroy and Lou Macari and I shall again for they really found their feet as Manchester United players as the season went on. Sammy was a terrific professional and Lou was a ducker and diver and adapted well to his new role in midfield. I expected no less of the pair of them because that's why I played them, of course. I wasn't surprised.

Other players in the side developed at a less obvious pace. Brian Greenhoff came into the season with the Player of the Year award but it was after this season when he really made his name. Sometimes good things come from accidents and his repositioning as a centre half was one of those. He was a fantastic interceptor of the ball. Gerry Daly really had a great first half of the season, it seemed like he was scoring penalty kicks every week.

The other obvious name to mention is Martin Buchan. I knew him from our international days together – he was a great player, a great leader, and was fantastic at either taking instructions or using his intuition and putting his own organisational skills to use. I knew what I had and knew what I was getting – he was his own man and in the nicest possible way he had a great self-assurance that bordered on arrogance. I remember going to Spain to Louis Edwards' house in Magaluf. We were sitting around the pool and Martin was strumming his guitar as he liked to. "You play that quite well," I told him. "Yes, I speak fluent French too," he said. All the lads were taking the piss out of him but they loved him. When taking the decision to name a new captain mid-season, it had to be Martin. He took the role seriously, and his responsibilities. He loved being in charge and did everything by the book, such as organising tickets for the players – never more than two each. He was the perfect and natural choice as a captain to lead this young team.

After the winter hiccup we responded so positively and it seemed like a case of 'so near, yet so far'. We were constantly on the verge of sealing promotion but it was never quite certain and so I was never fully confident of making future plans until it was mathematically done and dusted. In theory we were there – we put ourselves and the supporters through a nail biting Easter weekend when it seemed we could be promoted at any time. We were anxious to celebrate but we'd gone past the point of being worried that we wouldn't go up – though I'm sure the directors had one or two concerns about it dragging out.

Although I will never say I was happy to have taken Manchester United into the Second Division I am aware that a lot of people remember the time fondly. Ask me what my happiest memory of the Division was and I'll tell you it was getting out of it! Once I knew we were up, we could start making plans and adjustments for the future.

There is one thing you can never give someone, one thing you can never buy, and that's experience. My players had developed and grown up through the year and I had learned a lot too. The relegation meant that collectively – and I include myself in this – we had learned not to get carried away or ahead of ourselves with any success. We knew that someone would always be around to try and trip us up, and I knew that I was still two or three players away from what I ultimately wanted to see. There had been difficulties with some players and what I had learned from the events of the 1974/75 season as far as managing my team went was that I had to ensure, going forward, that I was aware of the character of players before I signed them. When a manager picks a player, particularly a young player, he's praised and is the best thing since sliced bread. For the player being dropped, the manager doesn't know what he's doing. That's a football problem, not a problem consigned to particular individuals. I knew that in order to achieve what I wanted to in the future, I had to ensure that players were aware that it was increasingly becoming a squad game and sometimes they may face a spell on the bench. Only Martin Buchan, the captain, was an automatic selection.

Personnel was one thing. Our win at Southampton saw us promoted and that meant I was able to permanently put into action a formation I'd wanted to use since signing Steve Coppell at the end of February, an attempt to better utilise or put into practice the philosophy I was hoping to see grow.

I'd always been brought up with wingers, and playing 4-2-4. I was brought up on two-touch football at Preston North End. Speed of movement, every morning. Push and run – just like Tottenham. Control, pass, control, pass. No need to tackle hard, just get in and nick the ball. This was not just the football I was brought up with but the football I loved to see and the style I wanted my team to play. The emphasis was very much on attack but responsibly so; it was a formation that looked gung-ho when it had the ball but could track back and shift when the opposition had it. I had tried to play it earlier with George Best and Willie Morgan but George was never a proper winger. When I signed Stevie Coppell we then made that our permanent formation because Stevie worked so hard, a great complement to the other three who were creative. Full backs who played against us didn't want to follow Coppell and then later Gordon Hill into the middle of the park because they knew they'd leave huge gaps and be embarrassed. They hated it.

We didn't have a hard or aggressive player in the team, but they were technically very skillful, and used their speed and energy to their advantage. It has been interesting to hear the thoughts of Brian Greenhoff, Sammy McIlroy and Gordon Hill, comparing our team to the Barcelona team which enjoyed so much success in recent years. Like the Barcelona side, we were like flies around a sugar bowl when the other team had the ball. We'd hurry them into making mistakes. Home and away we played the same way.

The football was great to watch – as I've already said, I enjoyed it as much as anyone, and so I can completely understand why the supporters remember the year with affection. It goes the same for the players too – so many found themselves this season that it is natural that they have a predilection for it too. Perhaps, for some supporters of an age able to remember the 1974/75 season, seeing the modern successes of Manchester United and the style in which they have mostly been accomplished has made them remember how we played with the same spirit.

This book chronicles the start of that journey faithfully. It provided a great trip down memory lane for me, and I hope it does for you supporters too.

Tommy Docherty

CALL THE DOC

IT SEEMS ALMOST UNTHINKABLE, looking back, that Manchester United spent the 1974-75 season in Division Two. The series of events which led to their relegation in 1974 would be almost inconceivable to a modern supporter. Mention 'regeneration' and a fan assumes that means one year of transition without challenging for the Championship or perhaps missing out on the Champions League. Mention 'give the manager time to build a new team' and that means adding two or three world class players to the squad he already has and giving him 6 months.

Tommy Docherty was not the man who directly followed Sir Matt Busby as Manchester United manager yet neither could he rightly be blamed for the situation the club found themselves in when they were relegated on 27th April 1974. It would be unfair to pin the entire demise on either Wilf McGuinness or Frank O'Farrell too - these were simply the wrong men at the wrong time, unable for whatever reason to handle the task of managing the 'Hollywood of Football', as Harry Gregg became fond of describing the club.

On December 16th 1972, United went down 5-0 to fellow relegation strugglers Crystal Palace. They were one point off bottom of the table Leicester City, who had a game in hand over them and yet the side that lost that day contained five of the players, Messrs Stepney, Dunne, Sadler, Kidd and reluctant substitute Denis Law, who had lifted the European Cup just 1,662 days earlier.

The purpose of this book is not to attribute blame for the rapid descent which saw United fall from the lofty perch of European Champions to Division Two, or to even explore that period. However it is important to acknowledge the role that the immediate past had in getting United to where they were in 1974/75 and writing it in the modern age it is impossible to do so without drawing contemporary parallels.

No, Docherty wasn't the man who immediately followed Busby, and he wasn't responsible for what he inherited, but he was responsible for making a number of tough decisions, principally handling the departures of three European Footballers of the Year in Bobby Charlton, Denis Law and George Best. He did so, and United were relegated, and it is hard to imagine that in the present era that his position would have been safe.

It has to be said that Tommy Docherty is one of the most important people in the history of Manchester United; the 'Doc' is often unfairly simply dismissed as a controversial rent-a-quote yet he is responsible for the rebirth and rebuilding of the club, setting the foundations on which Sir Alex Ferguson would build years later. Most of those who played under Docherty in 1977 insist that the days of Division One success and European glory were on the verge of returning to Old Trafford.

Whether or not that has any truth is one of the great what if's. Docherty himself expected to be sacked as he reflected upon the defeat to Manchester City on the evening after the game. He has spoken about that expectancy and how he had tentatively began to think about how that would impact on his managerial future, but the following day he was reassured in person by Busby himself who handed his fellow Scot a case of champagne and said "We'll give you the time."

It was a huge vote of confidence. Charlton and Law had left in the summer of 1973, and despite last chances given to Best, in early 1974 he was to leave United for the final time. It has long been documented that it is a fallacy that Law relegated United with his goal for City in the Manchester derby but it may as well have done in symbolism; the chain of events would lead to questions over the judgement of the manager to allow two players of that stature to leave, even if Charlton was well past his best.

Docherty said in his 1981 book 'Call The Doc':

"The glory days had gone and I had been called in to be the unpopular fellow. I'd have been a darn sight more unpopular had it not been for a wonderful gesture by Bobby Charlton for which I will always be grateful. Bobby had played well for me. Then he came to see me one day to tell me he wanted to retire... That was superb. He made my job very easy, because there would have come a time when I would have had to say to him, 'Bobby, I think it's time for you to hang up your boots.'"

The Doc went even further with his praise.

"I think looking back now that I should have appointed Bobby as my No. 2 at United."

Docherty believed that Charlton should have had the opportunity to succeed him when he was sacked in 1977.

"Why Bobby? Several reasons. He's a great fellow, knows the game inside out, and the managerial experience he gained at Preston North End would have stood him in good stead... It would have been tailor-made for them – the return of the favourite son. When I look at Bobby in terms of a United manager, I would have to look for something wrong – but I can't find anything."

Of Law, Docherty said :

"Denis had a year of his contract to run, and I suggested to him that as I was building for the future, I would be prepared to give him a free transfer. Now a lot of players are delighted to get a free. I've had players come to me and ask for a free so that they can get some money from their next club, under the counter, tax-free. Denis wasn't pleased – but he certainly wasn't surprised. When I recommended it to the board, Sir Matt Busby was against it. He thought Denis could do us a job for another year or so. But the club gave Denis £5,000 tax-free for the remainder of his contract for that year, and he got the free. He could have stayed if he had wished – his contract wasn't finished. He didn't have to go."

In preparation for this book, Docherty claimed to have no problem with Denis today – while not dishonest in his assertion that Law could have stayed in theory, in practice, the striker's position at the club had become untenable and he was left with no option but to find new employers.

The case of Best – as ever – was unique. He was given every chance, sometimes apparently against Docherty's better judgement, because at 27, he should have been at his peak. Brian Greenhoff, the young defender who would be named as United's Player of the Season in that relegation campaign, said of the Northern Irishman, "He would be given special treatment because he was George. But when he was playing in that last season, that wasn't George." Twelve appearances and just two goals illustrates the point.

Another person that Docherty fell out with along the way was Pat Crerand – part of the lament of not appointing Charlton as his assistant included what Docherty later described as a 'mistake' in hiring Crerand. It's fair to say that in the years that passed neither has had a kind word to say about the other but George Best credits Crerand with convincing him to at least try and make one final comeback.

"And although I wasn't sure about going back, he (Crerand) convinced me that Docherty was a proper United man, who would bring in new players to restore the side to its glory days and most importantly, that his team would play the United way," recalled Best in his autobiography 'Blessed'. Best was famously dropped for the FA Cup clash against Plymouth Argyle in January 1974 although the true account of events depends on who you believe. The end result was clear for all to see – Best was finished at Manchester United. He appeared to bear no grudges towards

Docherty, saying, "I've worked with the Doc at dinners. I think he is a funny man. But I also think he can be a bullshitter."

Docherty had made the unpopular calls, be they overdue or premature (Best himself conceded that he was far from the same player he once was), to build a 'new' United, and the suggestion around the team was essentially that they had played well, but hadn't managed to score as often as they should have.

Sammy McIlroy and Lou Macari ended the season as top scorers with a poor return of six goals each – for a short while, Alex Stepney, the goalkeeper, had been leading goalscorer by virtue of his short spell as the Reds' penalty taker.

McIlroy felt his very future at the club was on the line – at the start of the '73/74 campaign, he was thrust back into first team action just a few months after suffering extensive injuries in a car crash. It was a tremendous show of faith and ostensibly a great thing to be thought of so highly, yet the mental pressure McIlroy was under and his admittance that he was not yet physically recovered meant he could have been doing his career more harm than good.

"I needed to show the manager what I could do. The car crash had knocked me back, and at the time the club seemed to be in a whirlwind – players were coming in and going out so quickly under Tommy Docherty. You naturally think, 'Jeez, what's gonna happen to me?'" McIlroy admits now. "Personally I wanted to get ready and fit – with the crash causing lung injuries, it really did knock me for six and it was a bit of a worry. Leaving the club was something I had thought of but I was so determined to get back. I think I had a year on my contract and after such a difficult year in '73/74, I was so anxious to prove myself. I think that the anxiety could have had an effect on how things turned out for me earlier – Tommy had shown great faith in putting me into the team right at the start of the season but I was in no way ready. I knew that, I was nowhere near. I was working with the late Bill Foulkes on my fitness but my breathing wasn't right. I was out from January and had gone on a tour to Switzerland with the youth team in May... I played, and I was nowhere near ready. It really did take me back. My confidence was low because I knew I wasn't right. I was working and playing as hard as I could but I knew I wasn't right. It was difficult because the papers were obviously always mentioning players coming in and you'd think, 'Ooh dear,' but the light I had was that Tommy clearly wanted me to do well. The problem I had was that even though that was the case, because I wasn't ready, I wasn't doing myself justice. I had a fire inside me saying I wanted to get back but another side of me saying 'You ain't ready.' I was rushing myself because I wanted to show I was capable of doing what I did when I first broke into the team. It was a young team and maybe it was anxiety that was our biggest problem in '73/74. Denis and Bobby had left, Brian Kidd was on his way out, and George had the brief comeback that didn't work out. Tommy had handled a lot of change, he had belief he could do it, but he knew he needed a bit of luck."

As Docherty himself mentioned earlier in this book, George Graham had suffered with the pressure of following Charlton, and now, Brian Greenhoff was having the same tag given to him. As brilliant as he was, Willie Morgan was not quite the next George Best, and nor was McIlroy – of the many afflictions McIlroy was suffering from, the burden of the comparison was never one.

"To be honest, I never, ever took anything like that seriously," he insists. "George Best was my idol, the greatest thing I've ever seen on a football field, and the comparisons were simply because we both came from Belfast, end of story. George was a fantastic bloke, he helped me when I broke into the side. Obviously the press loved it but I mean it sincerely when I say it didn't bother me... between us, we never mentioned it. Believe it or not, George was a shy lad, and George was my idol so I would never dream of mentioning it. Rather than 'being him', a sad regret is that I didn't get to play as often with him as I could. Also to see him as he was at the end of his time at United wasn't great because it was so sad for a number of fans whose only memory of him is those last days, because that wasn't what he really was."

Perseverance with Best may also have exacerbated the lack of confidence from United's other forwards – yet it was still another bold decision by Docherty to take the decision to sell Brian Kidd in the close season. Kidd had scored just two goals in 24 games but at the age of 24 was still attractive enough to be signed by Arsenal for £110,000. He was deemed surplus to requirements because of a classic Docherty gamble – he spent £200,000 on Stuart Pearson from Hull City.

It was a lack of goals – just 38 in 42 games – which would ultimately prove to be United's undoing. Brian Greenhoff later said (perhaps underling the point made by McIlroy about anxiety), "We were trying to play the right way and sometimes we did play good football, but we lacked a cutting edge up front."

Martin Buchan, another of the few to escape from relegation with his reputation unscathed, agrees. "Our defensive record wasn't as bad as some of the teams that stayed up. For us, we just didn't score enough goals. I remember it being thought that we were too good to go down but I never thought that. Points on the board is all that matters."

United failed to score in 20 of 45 League and Cup games that season and while the absence of a potent goalscorer may explain a team's failure to challenge for honours, it cannot be acknowledged as the sole reason for a team like Manchester United to be relegated.

The Reds drew another blank in the derby against City as Law infamously struck with a nonchalant backheel. He didn't celebrate – indeed, he walked off the pitch, and could later be found with his head in his hands in the home dressing room. Gerry Daly later said in 'The Doc's Devils', "I wasn't too far away. I don't think he wanted to score."

Provoked by the goal, the supporters staged a pitch invasion. It has since gone down as another of those misreported 'myths' – with the hooligan culture rife in football, and United's fanbase being no different in that a section of its supporters were involved in trouble on occasion, it was suggested that the invasion was a last ditch attempt to get the game abandoned, and subsequently replayed. In actual fact, a pitch invasion was a tradition for the last home game of the season, as this was – but, with the frustration of events getting too much, supporters didn't wait until the game was over. With the availability of radios, they were well aware that events at Old Trafford were now essentially meaningless, so the last thing that the supporters would have wanted in all actuality would be for the game to have been replayed.

The police temporarily managed to clear the pitch and play resumed, but for less than five minutes before another invasion – Sir Matt Busby made announcements over the PA system asking for the fans to clear the pitch, but his attempts were in vain. Dave Smith, the match referee, decided to abandon play, with the Football League later ruling that the score should stand.

The only ones disappointed were United's players, who had hoped that they would at least save face by getting an equaliser and not suffering the ignominy of their last First Division game at Old Trafford ending in defeat. They were unable to atone for that in their final game in the division, losing 1-0 at Stoke City on the final day. United supporters were seen to burn scarves and programmes in the stands.

Any manager taking an institution like Manchester United into the Second Division would expect to face the axe so it was no surprise that Docherty had a moment of self doubt following confirmation of the drop. It's perhaps a little ironic that he was supported at such a crucial time by a number of senior figures who he would later be on far worse terms with when times were ostensibly good.

Busby's support was immediate while Pat Crerand had already gone on record by stating he felt Docherty was doing things the right way in spite of results; and Alex Stepney, the senior goalkeeper who at the age of 31 was never far from the manager's thoughts in terms of a replacement, was indeed positively gushing, and sympathetic, in his praise. "We were on our way down to the Second Division and yet, in all the adversity, Docherty was at his best," said Stepney in his 1978 eponymous autobiography. "He never went hiding. He was always there, telling us we could win when, deep down, he must have been desperately disappointed... Docherty said at the time that, no matter what happened in the future, he would be known as the man who took Manchester United into the Second Division. He was being a shade hard on himself at the time, for few people blamed him completely."

Brian Greenhoff was surprised but relieved that his mentor wasn't given the sack. "It's a miracle that he wasn't sacked," he admitted.

It is worth noting at this point that Docherty's self-confidence and bullish, outspoken reputation had preceded him. His decision to reprimand a number of senior Chelsea players by dropping them before a game at Burnley in 1965 had, it was commonly agreed, cost the Blues the chance of winning the First Division (ironically in a chase with United). He had a wise-cracking, controversial personality before he even arrived in Manchester and the process of events and path that led to him succeeding Frank O'Farrell in December 1972 suggest that in the summer of 1974, Docherty was feeling decidedly vulnerable and unsure. This much is confirmed by his thoughts documented earlier in this record.

After all, he had left what most of his countrymen would

consider the 'Holy Grail' of the Scotland national team manager's job to go to Old Trafford. It had been a dream of Docherty's for almost a decade – in 'Call The Doc', he wrote:

"I'd always felt that to manage Manchester United was my destiny… and the day I was appointed, I walked into the centre of the pitch in the empty ground, looked around me and hummed to myself 'You were meant for me'. And I added the next line of the lyric, too – 'I was meant for you,' because that's the way I felt. It's the only stadium in the world I've ever been in that's absolutely buzzing with atmosphere when it's empty and there isn't a soul inside. It's almost like a cathedral. To me, a Catholic, it's like going to Rome and walking into St Peter's Square. The whole place is soaked in history and atmosphere."

It's something of a surprise that Docherty didn't keep hold of that analogy for later repeating as it doesn't regularly appear in his repertoire, if at all. For in 1974, it would have probably been more apt to compare the state of United to Roman ruins.

United were of course already synonymous with life on the continent. In its relatively short life, European football had become part of the fabric of the club. Obviously, following relegation, United would not be featuring in any competitive football on the biggest stage but that did not stop them taking to the continent to prepare for life in the second tier. Nor did it stop them making the headlines.

PRE-SEASON

SATURDAY 3RD AUGUST 1974 - FRIENDLY

OSTEND 1-2 MANCHESTER UNITED

Stepney, Young, Houston, Greenhoff, Sidebottom, Buchan, McIlroy, Daly, Pearson[2], Macari, McCalliog

Nowadays it wouldn't be a surprise to see the season kick-off in the first week in August; indeed, with the saturation of European qualifiers, some clubs often find themselves with competitive football in July. Any suggestions that Manchester United would be having an easy year could be discounted quickly; 67 matches including cup-ties and friendlies would be played from August 3rd 1974 to June 24th 1975, as Tommy Docherty led his Red men on a world wide post-season tour.

Yet it was in the unfamiliar setting of Belgian seaside resort Ostend where United's preparation for life in Division Two began, and Stuart Pearson made an instant impression with two debut goals either side of a home equaliser. Later, Pearson may have scored a hat-trick, but that effort was disallowed.

The concentration of this book is primarily on the football but it would be wrong to dismiss the importance or, at least, relevance of the hooligan culture and the trouble that followed United in this season. While far from a problem that was solely confined to United, it played a prominent enough role for it to warrant being replayed through this journey back in time. There would be numerous discussions about this as the club dealt with it head on and proactively but the hysteria and provocation from the media was seen as concerning from those within the sport. That said, there could be no accusation of inventive reporting as trouble followed the Reds to their very first warm up game.

"Five British Soccer fans were handcuffed and taken to a fortress prison in the medieval town of Bruges yesterday. They will be joined soon by a sixth, at present held under police guard in an Ostend hospital," printed the *Daily Mail*. "The six – all Manchester United fans – will be held in jail until they are brought to trial following a drunken rampage by supporters through Ostend... 33 Manchester United supporters were held by police during riots before their club's game against AS Ostend on Saturday. But 27 were shipped home because they were under 18. The fuse to the rioting was lit on the cross-Channel ferry when hundreds of fans went on a drinking bout. About 1,200 travelled to Belgium but there were only 63 fans in the official party organised by supporters club chairman David Smith." The article later referenced trouble between Sunderland and Newcastle supporters while also saying 30 supporters were due in court after trouble in a game between Huddersfield and Leeds United – finally, 18 Manchester City fans would face a day in court after trouble in their game at Blackpool.

For some, the season represented a real coming of age. This was the case for United supporter Gary Thompson, who was fifteen and in his last year at secondary school. Gary's fond memories of the team are typical of the supporter base. "Like most kids of the time I had several favourite players. I'd say the three stand out ones were probably Sammy McIlroy, Gerry Daly and of course Brian Greenhoff. All players I would have liked to have emulated but failed miserably!" says Gary, who was also firmly in support of the manager despite the relegation. "Tommy Docherty had the United fans eating out of the palm of his hand, he was like a God. I think he's very much fondly remembered even to this day."

TUESDAY 6TH AUGUST 1974 – FRIENDLY

STÆVNET 0-1 MANCHESTER UNITED

Stepney, Forsyth, Houston, Greenhoff (Martin), Holton, Buchan, McIlroy, Daly, Pearson[1], McCalliog, Anderson

The match programme for this encounter featured a welcome from Vilh. Skousen who wrote "Our visitors will, no doubt, be keen to confirm the merit of their former good games here in Copenhagen and we will wish them the best of luck in the coming season at home, a season, I am convinced, will bring them back to earlier heights in English and international football." Elsewhere in the programme, Tommy Docherty was described in a profile as "facing all the adversity (he) could get, and relegation was a reality. The good thing about him is that he loves it. Quite simply. Football is his elixir."

Pearson made the difference again in this game against a composite side drawn from nine clubs in Copenhagen.

THURSDAY 8TH AUGUST 1974 – FRIENDLY

HOLSTEBRO 0-4 MANCHESTER UNITED

Stepney, Forsyth, Houston, Greenhoff, Holton, Buchan, McIlroy[2], Macari, Pearson (Anderson[1]), McCalliog[1+], Daly

After a keenly contested first period, United's class told in the second period as United romped home to victory. Unsurprisingly given the scoreline, Docherty described this as the best match of the tour.

HULL CITY 1-1 MANCHESTER UNITED

Stepney, Forsyth, Houston (Young), Greenhoff, Holton, Buchan, Morgan (McIlroy), Macari, Pearson[1], McCalliog, Daly

The Tigers saw this game as an opportunity to wish their former striker a fond farewell, explaining in the opponent's profile of the programme, "A chance for Tigers' fans to give him a rousing send-off to his career with his new club." Hull were equally gracious towards their visiting club, gushing over their achievements and then lamenting "Now, alas, the party is over. Manchester United must return for a while to the Second Division. And all of us are the losers. For have not Manchester United been - are they not still - the biggest draw in football for almost three decades?" and closing with the statement "The Second Division is no place for Manchester United. May they return to their rightful place with the minimum delay."

One player in particular was the recipient of special praise and, surprisingly, it wasn't their returning hero. "… they have hopes for several young players, particularly Brian Greenhoff, who for one of such tender years, has shown tremendous versatility. Whether he be playing centre forward, centre back or in midfield, Greenhoff always stands out. For all the world, here is another Bobby Charlton in the making."

There was no suggestion the hosts would stand on ceremony when the whistle went; they took the lead in the first half, before Pearson got the goal he so dearly wanted early in the second half to send everyone home satisfied.

An interesting subplot to the game came to light when it was revealed that Martin Buchan might not have even featured - the club had retained the players passports after the European trip, and Buchan protested that his passport was his private property.

"As we were collecting our luggage from the conveyer belt at Manchester airport after the pre-season trip, Tommy Cavanagh was going around all the players asking for their passports, saying they wanted to keep them at the club. I refused," says Buchan. "I said, "A passport's a valuable document. I'm a big boy, I know that the next time I'm going abroad I'll need my passport." Tommy said, "Yeah but some of the lads forget it." "I'm not some of the lads! Treat the ones that behave like kids that way but not me," I said. "Well you're not playing at Hull!" Tommy replied. "Fair enough."

"Of course I didn't want to miss the last of our warm-up games but I wasn't going to be bullied. It took Paddy Crerand to get involved, when I was at home he asked me to go and join up with the lads at Hull. I agreed on the condition I kept my passport. Maybe they'd had problems before but I thought it was an odd thing to ask. If it had been discussed among the group I might have been more open to it, because at that time of year we'd finished with any private or family holidays until the end of the coming season. It wouldn't have been a problem and I suppose it wasn't really a major problem, more much ado about nothing."

Buchan had been courted by top flight clubs throughout the summer but says he never had any intention of leaving. "When we got relegated there were First Division teams that wanted me and they all got the same message. I was one of the team that got Manchester United relegated and I'd be part of the team that brought them back up. That was how I felt about it."

And so, that was that. Four games in the space of eight days, one of those being an opponent they would face in the coming campaign, was enough to constitute a pre-season warm up. In the club's first official newsletter of the season they declared the pre-season a 'great success', deciding – wisely – to not pass comment on the controversy.

AUGUST

Sᴀᴛᴜʀᴅᴀʏ 17ᴛʜ Aᴜɢᴜsᴛ 1974 - Dɪᴠɪsɪᴏɴ Tᴡᴏ - Bʀɪsʙᴀɴᴇ Rᴏᴀᴅ (17,772)

LEYTON ORIENT 0-2 MANCHESTER UNITED

Stepney, Forsyth, Houston[1], Greenhoff, Holton, Buchan, Morgan[1], Macari (McIlroy), Pearson, McCalliog, Daly

It was said that there were supporters camping outside Brisbane Road the evening before the game for the opportunity to watch United's first game of the season. Just under 18,000 crammed into the ground with a reported 6,000 more locked out, which would become something of a familiar theme throughout the season. Orient were good opponents for United to gauge the difficulty of the task which lay ahead of them as the London-based outfit had missed out on promotion the previous campaign by a single point.

Jill Palmer of the *Evening Standard* was keen to point out there was some consolation for that in her Orient match-day programme column, saying "We could not go to the First Division, so it has almost come to us, in the shape of one of football's great names, Manchester United." Orient manager George Petchey also made mention of the opponents in his notes. "Today's attractive visitors Manchester United have won just about every honour in the game in their illustrious history," Petchey said. "I am confident that the team he (Docherty) is rebuilding will be competing for

Stewart Houston nets from close range at Brisbane Road

a place in the top three of the Division at the end of the season."

Incidentally, listed at number 12 on the match programme for the O's was seventeen year old Laurie Cunningham, who was profiled inside. "Orient manager George Petchey is certain his debut winger Laurie Cunningham is going to be a great player," it said. "And on the evidence of what I saw at Upton Park, Petchey could be spot on with that prediction." Cunningham would, of course, be signed by United on loan by Ron Atkinson years later to bolster the squad's front line.

The paucity of United's attack had been highlighted by Docherty's unusually conservative approach throughout most of the start of the '73/74 season. Sir Matt Busby had encouraged Docherty to be more positive but it wasn't until shortly after the signing of Jim McCalliog in March that the shackles came off. A comprehensive 3-1 win at Stamford Bridge had given the Reds what was to ultimately be vain hope but what it did do was instill a new, defiant attitude that quickly spread throughout the club. An injury to Steve James in that game against Chelsea meant Brian

Greenhoff had to move back into central defence but his attitude as a forward thinking distributor of the ball had a profound impact on the team's adventure. Docherty's line of thought – that if United were going to go down, they were going to down all guns blazing – was as admirable as it was ultimately ill-fated but it was this change in attitude which would forever change the way his teams would play and, in time, be remembered.

Greenhoff was back in midfield for the Second Division opener and just before the half hour, his searching through ball found the captain Willie Morgan who thrashed the ball into the Orient goal. United's class told on the day and they were able to contend with the abrupt and physical approach of their opponents – their second goal underlined the positivity of the game plan. With a quarter of an hour remaining, Alex Forsyth took a free kick that was met at the back post by a thundering Stewart Houston header which went in off the post. Only Martin Buchan of the outfield contingent had stayed back – the measured Scot was probably still trying to take in what he would later describe as the 'wild tackling' of the Second Division.

In the programme for United's second home game of the season against Portsmouth, *Manchester Evening News* journalist David Meek was forthcoming in his praise for the men involved in United's first goal.

"His (Morgan) goal in London was a cracker, splendidly created by Brian Greenhoff but magnificently scored by Morgan who with his ability and experience should be scoring much more frequently... Brian Greenhoff can also look ahead with confidence... he is next in line for the captaincy of Manchester United." Meek also recalled the words of Docherty in praise of the Barnsley-born utility man who was flavour of the month. "Brian has matured a lot since he came into the team. He is the right material to become a captain of the future."

The 2-0 result may have been just what was expected anyway but United still deserved some credit for the composed way in which they tackled what was a stern test to life in the Second Division. In many ways, the Reds would be in a no-win situation for the rest of the season. The expectation was such that they could have won every game and no-one would have blinked an eye but United still had to maintain composure and concentration if they wanted to turn their undoubted superior quality into results.

Crowd trouble continued to dog the Reds and it is debatable whether the good will extended to United by Orient prior to the game lasted for long afterwards. David Meek reported 'young United fans brought disgrace to the club on the trip to London'. There had been stories of a fight between United and Arsenal fans on London's Euston Road near St. Pancras station in the morning before the game.

Another 'c' word that was key to promotion chances and on the lips of many was confidence. Were United still feeling sorry for themselves? There was certainly a very sombre mood in the match programme for the first Old Trafford game of the season, where the Reds welcomed Millwall.

Louis Edwards :

"It makes me very sad to write a message for the first time as Chairman of a Second Division Club especially as it it some 36 years since we were last in this position. Undoubtedly last season was a big disappointment to the Directors, Manager, Players and staff and was a great blow to our supporters. I can only assure you that every possible effort is being and will be made by everyone at the Club to achieve of fortune and, if at all possible, to get back in the First Division at the first attempt."

Edwards then noted praise and criticism for the club's supporters.

"I would like to say again how much my colleagues and I appreciate the tremendous support given to us in the recent lean years. It is our aim to reward your great loyalty and enthusiasm by achieving that success we are all wanting and you our supporters deserve so much.

"One of the new features at Old Trafford and one we were very reluctant to put in are the fences behind each goal. You are all aware of the reason these have been put up and we earnestly hope that those spectators who came on to the pitch and caused our match versus Manchester City to be abandoned on the 27th April will appreciate the disgrace they have brought to our Club. Most of them were very young and possibly did not understand the seriousness of their actions but the older ones who went on the pitch must have known and should have realised the consequences. We have not put fences along the touchlines but if there is a move to the paddocks to get on the field from there then we will be forced to put them there also. We hope the adult supporters will discourage the youngsters from attempting to do this and that the youngsters will realise their actions reflect against the good name of the Club as well as themselves. We are grateful for your enthusiasm but would ask you to remember to do nothing that brings our Club into disrepute.

"I would now like to say a word to those supporters who travel to away matches. It seems to me that many of them think they are defending the honour of the Club when they cause trouble but all I can say is that there is no credit in being known as the worst behaved football followers in the country. At one time Manchester United supporters had the reputation of understanding and appreciating good football and were always ready to applaud it whether it was from their own team or our opponents. I am very sad when I admit that this reputation no longer applies to Old Trafford."

Docherty spoke passionately about United's chances and echoed his chairman's sentiments.

"Welcome back to Old Trafford and our new life in the Second Division. You, the fans, gave us tremendous support in our fight

against relegation and I am truly sorry that it did not bring a happier ending. But that battle is now history and I just hope that you will stay with us for the big challenge this season to win promotion. I think I can promise you that the staff and players will make every effort to give you more to cheer about this season. Everyone at Old Trafford is deeply conscious of the debt we owe you for your loyal support and it will be our inspiration in the months ahead. The question I am constantly asked now is whether we shall win back our place in the First Division at the first attempt. I would dearly like to answer that with an unqualified yes, but soccer has a nasty habit of wrecking bold predictions. So I am not going to tempt providence and say yes of course we will win promotion this season. What I can say is that everyone connected with the club will be working flat out to achieve it. I am also quietly confident because towards the end of last season I saw signs of real progress after a very unsettling period of rebuilding."

And then later :

"...The Chairman in his message today has referred to the people who cause trouble at away matches and I would like them to know that I fully agree with what he has said. We all appreciate the wonderful encouragement our genuine supporters give us at away games but a minority of hangers on, by getting involved in fights and causing damage to property and terrorising innocent people who happen to be in the vicinity, cause irreparable damage to the good name of Manchester United Football Club."

SATURDAY 24TH AUGUST 1974 - DIVISION TWO
OLD TRAFFORD (44,756)

MANCHESTER UNITED 4-0 MILLWALL

Stepney, Forsyth, Houston, Greenhoff, Holton, Buchan, Morgan, McIlroy, Pearson[1], Martin, Daly[3*]

In his column in the match day programme, David Meek proclaimed "Stuart Pearson makes his home debut for Manchester United this afternoon... the key figure in the Reds' bid to win back their First Division place". Those words may well have inspired the Yorkshireman who scored with less than five minutes on the clock - from that point, United were able to lay down a marker in their first home game with a comprehensive home win. Pearson was able to intercept a backpass, beat his marker and then round the goalkeeper to instantly win over the home support and ease some of the burden of his price tag.

Lining up against United on match-day was a young forward tipped for greatness. Gordon Hill - who, 15 months later, would be signing for the Reds - was described as a 'very good prospect' in the programme. United went on to score three more times with a hat-trick from Gerry Daly which included two penalties in the last ten minutes but there was no suggestion that the scoreline was not a fair reflection of the divide between the sides. Hill later admitted, "We were the Lions but we were slaughtered that day."

Visiting boss Benny Fenton warned future visitors to Old Trafford. "A lot of teams will come here to find such an atmosphere a completely new experience. It affects players. It can drain away all their energy," he said after the game.

The crowd trouble at Orient was enough to warrant a mention in Docherty's notes for the following home game which came

Stuart Pearson opens his United account against Millwall

just four days later with United looking to seek to build on the momentum from their fine start. He had explained in his notes for the Millwall game, "Some of our games on away grounds will be like cup finals for atmosphere and motivated opponents."

When it came to the programme for the Portsmouth game, Docherty noted, "The attendance at Orient was much lower than expected and I think a lot of local people stayed away for fear of trouble, which is another sorry state of affairs for soccer. It was commented on in the Press that I had banned my own boy from attending away matches. This actually is a slight exaggeration... what I have done is to warn him like any other parent... I certainly agree it is sad when a man of the game like myself has to start warning his own boy away from football."

His programme notes were once again dominated by references to the trouble and included just a minor note at the end to say, "Meanwhile we extend a hearty welcome to Portsmouth this evening and look forward to the game."

WEDNESDAY 28TH AUGUST 1974 - DIVISION TWO - OLD TRAFFORD (42,547)

MANCHESTER UNITED 2-1 PORTSMOUTH

Stepney, Forsyth, Houston, Greenhoff, Holton, Buchan, Morgan, McIlroy[1], Pearson, Martin, Daly[1+]

There could be no concerns about Portsmouth being afraid of the reputation of their opponents as they played with a conservative attitude, determined to steal a point. Coupled with United not quite being at their stellar best, for long periods it seemed as if the visitors might get a share of the spoils. When United were awarded a penalty, Gerry Daly kept up his 100% record of the season with a determined finish. Sammy McIlroy got his first of the campaign to finally force the visitors to come out to play; when they converted a late penalty of their own, they might have wondered what might have been if they had been more positive, but it was too little too late and the result was enough to put United second in the table behind Fulham on goal average.

McIlroy said that it was the opponents bowing to a relentless attack rather than patience in the home side – and was naturally delighted to get a goal under his belt. "It was a boost to score and win the game but we knew that teams were going to come and do what Portsmouth did," he says. "We thought, 'bloody hell we'll have to break down a nine man defence here'... but then, it wasn't as if we had any patience. It was so swift. It wasn't as if the Doc just sent us out there, we played as a team and wanted us to have the ball as often as possible."

Hooliganism was the talk of the programme notes again for United's game against Cardiff City but, showing it wasn't a problem confined to M16, this time it was the hosts who used their match-day publication to condemn their own supporters.

"Incidents in Bristol early last week after our League Cup match at Ashton Gate brought us national publicity of a most unwelcome kind. We, Cardiff City Football Club, wish to make it clear that we are sickened and appalled by what happened... This afternoon we can, indeed must, start repairing the damage with a trouble-free 90 minutes."

United, meanwhile, set about a bold initiative to tackle their problem. Alex Stepney asked David Smith, the secretary of the Supporters' Club, to invite supporters to meetings at Old Trafford on Sunday mornings. "We want to guide them and let them know that they are letting us all down. I believe they will listen to us and that we will be able to get through to them," Stepney said. Details of that first meeting were revealed in the programme notes for the game against Nottingham Forest later on – "Forty United supporters met club captain Willie Morgan and Alex Stepney at Old Trafford on September 1 (last Sunday) at the invitation of the Supporters Club for talks aimed to bring peace on the terraces. All 40 fans had travelled to the away match at Cardiff and after being introduced to the club chairman, Mr. Louis Edwards, director Sir Matt Busby and manager Tommy Docherty they agreed to observe three requests from the players and the club : (1) Walk, not run, to and from grounds. (2) Walk away from taunts by rival fans. (3) Tell friends how the players they follow are upset by the behaviour of a minority of hot-heads. Willie Morgan said afterwards: "I would like to feel that we have made a worthwhile impression on the fans as a result of this meeting."

Docherty said he felt the first meeting was a success. "Everything is worth trying if it can help stop the present wave of trouble. The first visit went well and I think we shall hold more of these clinics."

The Bluebirds had not seen anything from their visitors that prevented them from offering anything other than a flattering welcome. "United: still the biggest draw of all" they explained.

"United are, in so many ways, unique. Who but Manchester United even in their relegation season could end up as the best supported team in the First Division with a gross aggregate attendance of 896,958 – 8,000 more than Liverpool... and who else but Manchester United could bring a trio of World Cup stars to glamorise the Second Division (Holton, Morgan and Buchan)."

SATURDAY 31ST AUGUST 1974 - DIVISION TWO - NINIAN PARK (22,344)

CARDIFF CITY 0-1 MANCHESTER UNITED

Stepney, Forsyth, Houston, Greenhoff, Holton, Buchan, Morgan, McIlroy, Pearson (Young), Martin, Daly[1+]

Despite Stuart Pearson's twentieth minute withdrawal through injury, United were able to secure a victory that took them to the top of the Division for the first time. Gerry Daly's fourth successful penalty in three games meant that the club had already scored more spot-kicks than they had the whole of the previous year! David Meek praised Daly's 'confident work' and said "The incredible thing is that he has sent the goalkeeper the wrong way on each occasion; and there is no simple solution for opposing goalkeepers either because he varies the side."

Docherty later expressed his own satisfaction of the performance in South Wales, feeling his team deserved to win by more. "....I thought Ron Healey, the former Manchester City goalkeeper, played particularly well in keeping us to a 1-0 win," the Doc wrote in his pre-match column ahead of the next home game. "What pleased me was that we still kept our pattern of play, going forward all the time and stringing our passes together to create good football, I also believe is entertaining."

This was a personal reward for Docherty and some early

The Red Army invade Wales

vindication for his labour although it was still too early to ascertain whether the cost in terms of stature and personnel had been worth it. Docherty calculated the turnover in his reign at 34 players earlier in the season and only now was he fielding something like a side that would resemble one which bore his hallmark. In fact, such was the turmoil at the club that reasonable voices even opined that relegation could have turned out to be the blast of fresh air that the club sorely needed. Martin Buchan said, "It gave Tommy Doc a chance to get rid of some of the dead wood at the club. It got the players into the habit of winning and I think the support increased because we were winning... but it was never as easy a season as Lou Macari used to say." Macari's words? "After five games where we'd banged in four or five goals in each game the penny dropped with us all that it was going to be a formality."

In an interview for this book, Macari revisited that opinion to clarify. "Because we were winning – and being a team that had dropped down a division, we were expected to – as the season went on, we got more confidence," he said. "It breeds the feeling that wherever we went, we were invincible. It's difficult for today's generation to appreciate or realise. We used to travel with thousands and thousands to away games, they'd be waiting for us when we got to these grounds. If they didn't have tickets then they were climbing over walls or getting into the ground by whatever means possible such was the desire and determination to see the team play. If they are going to such extremes then you have to think that they were doing that because they felt that we were on our way to becoming a good side and they were proven to be right."

Buchan's thoughts made plenty of sense – momentum and confidence can count for so much in football as in all sport and for a team whose own self-belief must have been shattered, to win in the style they had seen was not only encouraging to the supporters who were watching it, but to the players who were so desperately in need of that shot in the arm. Alex Stepney went on record to note the marked change in the demeanour of the boss. "When we kicked off in the Second Division and struck instant success I saw him change before my eyes," said Stepney in his 1978 book. "As we hit the top of the table the arrogance that had been subdued suddenly took over and he began to strut about with the aloofness of a game cock. He seemed to step away from Sir Matt whom he had previously courted avidly. He was still changing the team, looking for other players, trying youngsters and, to be fair to him, developing an attractive style of play that was much more along traditional United lines."

Pearson and Greenhoff may have shared the plaudits as United settled into the new season but there was no doubting who the man of the moment was and he was loving every minute of it. "It took for everybody. Everybody seemed to be playing well. We were a young side. We were enthusiastic. Everybody wanted the ball" Daly commented of the time in the book 'Doc's Devils'. The *Daily Mail's* Brian Scovell wrote "Manchester United showed enough class to indicate their stay at the top of Division Two will be a long one... with their new found confidence and their non-stop running, Tommy Docherty's men are quite obviously in the right mood to fight their way back into the top table at the first attempt." Another report said United were 'decidedly fortunate' to get a win at Ninian Park, saying the 'old magic had faded'.

Sadly, pleas for the game to pass without incident were once again ignored by a minority – 55 arrests were made after the game, though only 5 of those arrested were from Manchester. Not that United's followers would be portrayed as victims in reports.

"Welder Roy Jenkinson, 20, was one of the first to scramble on to the 8.30am train at Piccadilly. He spent most of the four-hour journey to Cardiff baiting British Transport Police who were making sure no one smashed up the carriages. 'Where's your bottle' he taunted at a young PC on the train. 'You ought to be charged extra for taking up the whole compartment' he jeered at another portly, bearded PC. When he drew breath it was to describe to his young admirers what he was going to do to the Cardiff City supporters," wrote reporters Ian Smith and Christopher White in a column they also explained that Cardiff supporters had chanted 'Munich, Munich' at United fans and that one young United follower – approximately 18 years old – suffered a knife wound to his arm, which multiple reports stated was 'a hair's breadth' from his artery. For some, escaping the long arm of the law was part of the thrill of the away games although these days many are all too eager to confess that United supporters were no angels. "I remember the mayhem at Cardiff especially... That was a bit of an eye opener to say the least," admits Gary Thompson. "But if you ask me was I aware of the controversy and the reputation of United's support in those days? Of course, I was part of it! I think you'd have to be a bit numb not to have been aware of all the goings on."

SEPTEMBER

WEDNESDAY 4TH SEPTEMBER - INTERNATIONAL FRIENDLY - OLD TRAFFORD (8,065)

MANCHESTER UNITED 0-2 REPUBLIC OF IRELAND XI

Stepney (Roche), Forsyth, Houston, Greenhoff, Sidebottom, Buchan (Nicholl), Morgan (Kelly), Anderson (Botham), McCreery, Young, Sutcliffe

Gerry Daly's compatriots were the visitors for this encounter as Johnny Giles – the former United forward and now manager of the Irish national team – brought a squad over to face a Reds team filled with senior faces for what was described by the *United Review* as an 'International Friendly Match'. United player Mick Martin was the scorer of both goals for his country in what was a disappointing outing.

Despite a number of first teamers getting minutes under their belt, opportunities were given to a couple of youngsters, including the 17 year-old Peter Sutcliffe and 16 year-old David McCreery who was described by Joe Lancaster in the 'Reserves' section of the Portsmouth programme as 'talented' with 'time on his side'. With an average age of just 24 (Alex Stepney at 31, and Willie Morgan at 29, the elder statesmen) in their line-up against Nottingham Forest the following weekend, the same could easily have been said of McCreery's team-mates.

Docherty certainly thought so as he welcomed Forest to Old Trafford. "A drop in division can often give young players the chance to find their feet and develop their match skills that they would find hard to produce in the First Division," Docherty wrote. "This is particularly applicable to Manchester United because we have a very young side by League standards and two or three of the players joined English football comparatively late in their careers."

Saturday 7th September - Second Division - Old Trafford (40,671)

MANCHESTER UNITED 2-2 NOTTINGHAM FOREST

Stepney, Forsyth, Houston, Greenhoff[1] (Macari), Holton, Buchan, Morgan, McIlroy[1], Martin, McCalliog, Daly

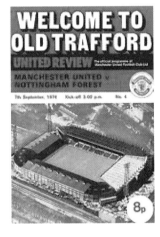

Unaffected by the slight friendly hiccup, United begun this encounter with all the style heralded by Docherty pre-match. Their attacking start was rewarded when Brian Greenhoff smashed his side into the lead. Forest settled and provided a stern test for the hosts, boldly attacking and testing their defence in an attitude not yet seen by visiting teams this term. Their adventure brought reward – goals either side of the break put them in command of the game and asked the first real question of United this season.

United's cause was not helped by an injury to Greenhoff but his replacement, Lou Macari (making his own comeback and his first appearance since the opening day) was a more than able attacking replacement. With time almost up, a draw was rescued by the tricky feet of Sammy McIlroy – the midfielder's effort from the edge of the area salvaged a point that kept United at the top of the Division.

No sooner had Second Division action resumed than distractions of another kind popped up; Third Division Charlton Athletic arrived for a Second Round League Cup tie. "Midweek fixtures at the end of a season if you are running for honours can be a burden," stated Docherty. "But the League Cup is all over by March 1. I just hope we can retain our involvement to that late stage. We shall certainly be trying because this is one of the ways into serious European competition that are still left open to us."

The match programme for the Charlton game also featured a very unusual contribution. As was the norm, the club invited supporters letters, but one correspondence sent in was as follows –

"QUOTE FROM NEWS OF THE WORLD, 25TH AUGUST, 1974.

"I always knew there would be a murder at a match. I thought it would happen at Manchester United."

CHIEF CONSTABLE, STANLEY PARR

"When I read the supposed quote in "The News of the World*" which was quite wrong, I intended to drop you a line to say so but it has been rather a busy week. Please assure your Directors that the quote is purely journalistic licence and never at any time was Manchester United or any other Club mentioned by name,"* PARR, LANCS. CONSTABULARY, PRESTON."

The letter referred to the incident on 24th August 1974 in a game between Blackpool and Bolton Wanderers when a 17 year-old Blackpool fan, Kevin Olsson, was stabbed to death.

Meanwhile, Docherty appeared to relent somewhat in his criticism towards United supporters. "We never seemed to have any bother at Old Trafford. I'm sure that on occasions when we were travelling, fans at the other end put on red and white colours just to stir up trouble." There could be no accusation of the clubs next visitors wearing red and white to cause problems!

WEDNESDAY 11TH SEPTEMBER - LEAGUE CUP SECOND ROUND
OLD TRAFFORD (21,616)

MANCHESTER UNITED 5-1 CHARLTON ATHLETIC

Stepney, Forsyth, Houston[1], Martin, Holton, Buchan, Morgan, McIlroy[1], Macari[2], McCalliog, Daly *
Unused Sub: Young

Perhaps encouraged by the reward that Forest had received for a positive attitude, the Addicks caused a huge shock to the half empty Old Trafford when Peter Hunt stole through to score in under a minute. One of the many footballing clichés is that you can score too early and that was the case here - the goal simply provoked an instant response from United, and the Londoners quickly folded. Before the quarter hour mark, Docherty's team had stormed into a 3-1 lead, with McIlroy and Macari scoring either side of an own goal. Houston and a second for Macari sealed a comprehensive result and put United in the hat for the next round. These were Macari's first goals of the season following a difficult first year at United.

A handsome win it may have been, yet some remained unconvinced. Journalist Alan Clifford wrote, "Much has been written about United's five-goal, midweek romp against Charlton. I prefer to regard that as an isolated match. Because in every other game played so far, United have enjoyed one of those spells when everything falls into place, the passing, teamwork, telepathic reading of the next move and so on. But it has not been sustained to the point where it matters most - within shooting distance of the opposition goalkeeper."

In fairness to Clifford, the assessment could well have been written at the end of the preceding season considering it was a fair summary of United's performances, only, they were now facing a lower standard of opposition. The above statements were justification to a piece entitled 'The team with 40,000 Players' where Clifford claimed, "If United's brand of football is not good enough to win promotion, then their raucous, massive following will almost certainly do the job for them!" and then sharing that another Second Division manager had told him that the Reds were guaranteed 40 points "by virtue of opposing sides going to pieces under the pressure of the Old Trafford roar".

Next up for Docherty's boys was a trip to twelfth-placed

West Bromwich Albion, who had won two and lost two of their four games so far. The manager was able to consider one of his favourites, Brian Greenhoff, for selection – the youngsters leg injury against Nottingham Forest was not serious enough to rule him out of contention against Charlton, but Docherty had decided against using him. In the end, he was only named as a substitute at West Brom, and despite the plaudits and the goal against Forest, Greenhoff's form was becoming indifferent. He put this down to a complacency in feeling like he'd earned a regular spot but resolved to train harder and put that across in games too. Additionally, he had just started wearing contact lenses. "It was like seeing real life in high definition, for the first time I could see things clearly... I thought I could before. It still took a while to get used to," admitted Brian.

Like the other sides United had travelled to, West Brom had plenty to say about their opponents illustrious recent history, listing all of their major trophies and then exclaiming 'in a matter of lines, you have honours galore'.

Saturday 14th September - Division Two - The Hawthorns (23,721)

· WEST BROM 1-1 MANCHESTER UNITED

Stepney, Forsyth, Houston, Martin (Greenhoff), Holton, Buchan, Morgan, McIlroy, Pearson[1], McCalliog, Daly

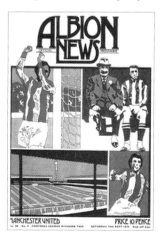

Once again United were slow out of the blocks – conceding in the sixth minute – before Pearson's 31st minute goal (struck with the instinct that had made him so appealing to Docherty) earned them a point. Greenhoff returned to action on the hour mark but within seven minutes was stretchered off after a collision which left him concussed. After treatment, he was sent back on, but had to come off again for further treatment before returning. "He was determined to go back on," wrote Docherty in his programme notes for the next home game, against Bristol City. In those same notes, Greenhoff's selflessness for the team was also revealed. "I sent to speak to Brian and he said he had intended coming to see me anyway because he did not see how it would be fair to split Mick Martin and Jim McCalliog after the way they played in the League Cup," Docherty revealed. "He made my job really easy because he was already looking at the problem from the point of view of the team and not just himself."

As effusive as Docherty was in his praise for the team spirit of both Greenhoff and the overall group, he was arguably using his column to breathe new fire into his team.

MONDAY 16TH SEPTEMBER - DIVISION TWO - THE DEN (16,988)

MILLWALL 0-1 MANCHESTER UNITED

Stepney, Forsyth, Houston, Greenhoff, Sidebottom, Buchan, Morgan, McIlroy, Macari, McCalliog, Daly[1+] (Young)

A fifth penalty of the season (and a third against Millwall) for Gerry Daly was enough to separate the sides, though the Lions did come close to snatching a point when future United winger Gordon Hill rattled the Reds crossbar. The home programme had a fairly provocative introduction to their 'welcome' with this lead in : "Probably at no time in the history of football has the name of one Club excited so much interest and comment as our 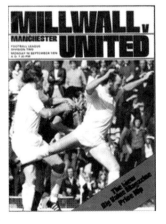 visitors this evening, MANCHESTER UNITED, particularly over the last thirty years. That is why it is so sad that a minority of so called United Supporters have by their alleged actions dragged the name of this famous club through the mire."

Such talk was almost delicious in its irony given the reputation that Millwall supporters had even then. Indeed, they were so outraged by the perceived injustice of the penalty award and other decisions they believe had not been given fairly, referee Ray Toseland was required to have a police escort from the field.

Lions boss Benny Fenton was slightly more diplomatic than the editor of the welcome notes to the programme but if understanding the sentiment, still had a different opinion from Leyton Orient's wish of United returning 'to their rightful place with the minimum delay'. "I would feel it goes without saying that most everyone in football would like to see them back in Division One as soon as possible, because they have so much to offer in the way of amenities, crowd drawing power and a tradition that is world wide," he wrote. "Having said that we will be doing our best to keep them in the Second Division, as will all clubs, because clubs in our division stand to gain so much, as apart from the obvious financial gains, the prestige to be gained by lowering their colours is enormous. Yes indeed football has a lot to thank Manchester United for." If Millwall were disappointed to see their clashes with United over as early as mid-September, the authorities probably breathed a sigh of relief.

An interesting observation to be made in the programme notes for the game against Bristol Rovers was that Docherty explained he felt that Willie Morgan was yet to 'hit the kind of consistency' he showed the previous year. "The eye operation at the beginning of pre-season training has obviously delayed his progress," observed Tommy. Of course, later on, the disagreements between the two would result in a court room drama. Still, it's interesting to note that Docherty's concerns about his compatriot's recovery were certainly very real at the time.

Another more humorous contribution to the match programme was a letter from the supporter Eric F. Marks from Prestwich who wrote "Old Trafford is surely one of the best grounds in the country with cantilever stands, electric scoreboards, private boxes etc. It lacks just one thing, a simple clock. Surely the provision of an electric clock at one end of the scoreboard would not tax the resources of the Club too much?" The editor responded "Passed on to Old Trafford for consideration but remember, the Referee is the sole time-keeper and his decision is the one that counts."

The Doc's pre-match notes for the Bristol game included a thought that he was pleased there was 'an abundance of character' in the team from their recent form and in particular the result from a hard fought game at West Brom. Even if Greenhoff was happy to concede to some complacency that wasn't something that could be levelled at his team mates and they did indeed deserve some praise for their resolute performances on the road but perhaps Docherty was hopeful that a home game would be enough to get some of the swagger back. Prior to the game, Docherty received a huge bottle of Bell's Whisky in recognition of his Division Two manager of the month award for August. "Just the first of many we hope," said the club's official newsletter. "But just one question, what would a Scotsman do with all that whisky?"

SATURDAY 21ST SEPTEMBER - DIVISION TWO - OLD TRAFFORD (42,948)

MANCHESTER UNITED 2-0 BRISTOL ROVERS

Stepney, Forsyth, Houston, Greenhoff[1], Holton, Buchan, Morgan, McIlroy, Macari, McCalliog (Young), Daly *

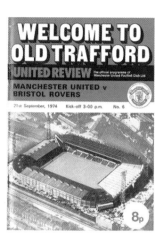

Whatever the reason, the swagger most certainly returned, with spectators unfortunate not to witness a six or seven goal landslide in what was arguably their most thrilling display of the season so far. United hit the woodwork on three occasions, but had to settle for just two goals in the end. Visiting manager Don Megson said "It must be obvious to anybody that they are going to take a lot of stopping."

One of those to be denied by the frame of the goal was Macari. David Meek wrote of the former Celtic man, "Macari is having a frustrating season... he scored twice in the League Cup tie but still had to make way for the return of Pearson". United took the lead early on through a Brian Greenhoff strike on nine minutes – and took a two goal advantage into half time when Gerry Daly's off-target effort was deflected in by Rovers defender Prince. United eased up in the second period, with their fine first half display enough to get the result.

The first newsletter of the season reported that the evening after the Bristol Rovers game, an 'Early Season Dance' for supporters was held at Belle Vue. In attendance were Louis Edwards and Denzil Haroun, as well as Tommy Docherty, who presented the Player of the Year award for 1974 to the also present Jim Holton. "Apart from an early evening 'Bomb scare' we feel quite certain that everybody in attendance thoroughly enjoyed themselves," it was noted.

Though there was very much a settled look to Docherty's preferred side these days, injuries and suspensions caused reshuffling and the manager was faced with a similar conundrum as he had with Brian Greenhoff; Macari had many attributes and on song was clearly one of the best players at the club, the dilemma was, where could he be played that would bring the best out of both him and the team?

WEDNESDAY 25TH SEPTEMBER - DIVISION TWO - OLD TRAFFORD (47,084)

MANCHESTER UNITED 3-0 BOLTON WANDERERS

Stepney, Forsyth, Houston[1], Greenhoff, Sidebottom, Buchan, Morgan, McIlroy, Macari[1], McCalliog, Daly *

As is the norm with these things – as sure forty or fifty years ago as it is today – as soon as Macari's contribution been called into question, he was smashing in a thumper of a volley to put United on their way to another comprehensive win in front of the biggest crowd of the season. The Trotters came to Manchester low on confidence and in the relegation zone but their neighbours took no sympathy on them whatsoever.

Houston then rifled in a free kick that was awarded for an incident involving Greenhoff on the edge of the area that looked as if it should have been a penalty – Docherty had mischievously quipped that the number of penalties his team had been awarded was actually stopping referees from giving them more, and in this game alone, there had already been one call before the man in black, Robert Perkin, gave the free kick which put the result beyond doubt. Just after the hour mark, Morgan's cross was headed in to his own goal by Bolton defender Don McCallister.

One member of the Bolton back line was familiar to every Red – Tony Dunne, who was actually making his second Old Trafford appearance in a matter of weeks, having been recalled to the Irish team for the friendly earlier in September. United did not make it a particularly warm return for the European Cup winning left back but Tommy Docherty did reserve special praise for the veteran in his match notes. "Tony has been back to Old Trafford for his testimonial and he could probably have been forgiven if he had decided that his glamour days were over and contented himself with taking things easy in the second string (at Bolton). But Tony Dunne has always been a first-rate professional and he has literally forced his way back into the reckoning... He was always a quiet player, but his attitude has been right and he has set a splendid example for young players in the game... I have no doubt it will be a highlight for him and he has provided a lesson worth nothing by players of all ages." Dunne was equally complimentary after the game, saying, "The atmosphere was as great as it ever was. United are easily they best team we have played this season... Young players like Sammy McIlroy, who used to be among the boys when I was at Old Trafford, have now blossomed and United's class is really showing."

"Their win against busy, bustling Bolton was clearly their best yet in the Second Division," wrote Ronald Crowther, disregarding the poor standing of opposition, but also giving credit to the Old Trafford support. "The fans who had never lost faith in United turned up in force again in a huge 47,084 crowd that put so many First Division attendances to shame."

After the 3-0 win that put his team five points clear at the top of the league, Docherty urged a little caution in an attempt to rein in any over-confidence. "It's great for the lads to be winning again but we mustn't get our heads in the clouds," he said. The author resists the strong urge to make some poor joke about coming face to face with Canaries while they were up there, but in United's next league game, they came crashing down to Earth.

NORWICH CITY 2-0 MANCHESTER UNITED

Stepney, Forsyth, Houston, Greenhoff, Sidebottom, Buchan, Morgan (Young), McIlroy, Macari, McCalliog, Daly

The pleasantries afforded to United were once again extended by Tony Pullein of the Canaries' programme, saying, "Manchester United are on their way back to the First Division! From the evidence of their performances so far, it is clear that few

clubs are going to get the better of them." The hosts may well have had cause to feel sorry for themselves considering they had lost 4-0 to Fulham the previous week but a creditable scoreless draw at high-flying Sunderland had kept them in third, five points behind the Reds and the Cottagers.

At Carrow Road, John Bond had his team playing free-flowing football and had in his arsenal the firepower of Ted MacDougall. MacDougall, formerly of United, had been sold by Docherty and, as is par for the course with the Doc, there was no love left between the two, and with all of the ingredients for the game nicely prepared, there was every incentive for MacDougall to inspire his team to victory. Predictably, it was the former United forward who made the difference, scoring both of Norwich's goals as the visitors relinquished the last remaining unbeaten record in the country to a first half penalty and an opportunistic back heeled goal which instantly drew comparisons to a similar goal scored by another Docherty outcast five months earlier.

United were unchanged from the team that had beaten Bolton so convincingly but were unable to beat Norwich stopper Kevin Keelan on the day. David Meek later reported that the Reds "created just as much danger near goal as their opponents and on the day the scoring luck was with the Canaries' though with the shaky performance of Sidebottom (who had kept his place due to Holton serving the second game of his two match suspension) partly to blame, their substandard defensive display meant that their inability to finish at the other end was punished in the most costly of ways."

The Norwich programme included a 'League Bulletin' which, surprise surprise, discussed hooliganism in the sport but with a curious approach. "The management committee has spent considerable time discussing the problems which have been caused by the increase in hooliganism and bad behaviour generally by youths who, while not being football supporters, profess to be so for the purpose of causing trouble," explains the bulletin, describing the troubles as a "major social problem" and then later suggesting that "Football League clubs have every right to feel that they have not been helped by the communications media... the Management Committee are firmly of the opinion that the glorification by the media of the offenders is a contributory cause of the increase."

With the nature of the two managers, there was always bound to be some sort of controversy after the game and if not particularly ungracious, Docherty responded unfavourably to the suggestion he had made the wrong decision in allowing MacDougall to leave. "I still think he (MacDougall) can't play," Docherty insisted. Bond took the bait. "I'm willing to bet right here and now that Ted will score twice as many goals this season as Macari," he boldly declared. It was hardly crisis point for the Reds; the defeat reduced their five-point lead to three with the knowledge that the Norwich away game was now out of the way, but the following game promised to be every bit as thorough an examination - fifth-placed Fulham at Craven Cottage.

In September, United were boosted by the news that revered

coach Frank Blunstone was to remain in charge of the Youth Team despite a lucrative offer from First Division Chelsea to become their first team manager following the Blues' sacking of Dave Sexton. "Some people will say that I'm either mad or frightened," Blunstone admitted to the Club's newsletter *There's only One... U-NI-TED.* "(But it's) Nothing of the sort. I happen to love the job I'm doing at Old Trafford. I like working with young players, it's one of the most exciting and important jobs in any club which can save thousands, perhaps even £1 million for the club over a period of years. I was manager at Brentford for four years and I therefore know a little bit of what is involved in that sphere of the game. During that time I was forever conscious of how vital each result was and in such an atmosphere it is impossible to even consider changing the overall pattern of the way the game should be played in an effort to instill the kind of football that one believes is right. I have strong views on the way football should be played. Attacking, entertaining football is my game and as I've pointed out previously my present position enables me to put my ideas into practice without worrying too much about the result. I'm not at all interested in personal glory, and I think I proved that when I resigned from Brentford to join Tommy Docherty at United to take over the Youth managership. That I even considered the Chelsea offer was purely and simply a matter of loyalty to a club with whom I had been associated for seventeen years as a player, during which time I enjoyed a tremendous relationship with everyone connected with the club. I can state quite honestly that had any other club than Chelsea made the offer to me I would have dismissed it immediately.

"In turning down the opportunity I must say that I felt it a great personal honour to have even been considered for the position, but after taking everything into consideration there was only one answer I could have given. Job satisfaction is more important to me than financial reward and after only twelve months with Manchester United I know that my decision to join them and to stay with them will prove the right one in time to come. Manchester United are on their way back to glory again and I have intense loyalty to them particularly after the way they stood by me when they kept my position open while I lay helpless following a serious car accident shortly after my appointment as Youth Team Coach. Throughout Manchester United there is a special aura that has to be experienced to be believed. Manchester United is not just a football club, it is an institution and to be associated with them is something very special.

"My family are very happy in Manchester and both myself and my wife, Doreen, will always remember that huge bunch of red and white carnations we received from the Southampton Branch of the supporters club after my decision to stay was announced. I think proof that I made the correct decision can best be illustrated by the attitude of my 16-year-old daughter Corina. When I first came to Manchester United she was somewhat upset at leaving London and her many friends. So when the papers published the Chelsea details I expected her to be in favour of a return south. But it wasn't the case. As soon as I arrived home she said, 'Dad, if you go to Chelsea and we move back to London, I'm returning to Manchester every weekend for the match.' That is what Manchester United does to you - believe me."

While there is no doubting the sincerity of Blunstone's words it is nonetheless interesting that later on, when interviewed for the book 'The Doc's Devils', he offered a slightly less romantic version. "I went down to see the chairman of Chelsea. 'Could I start on the Monday?' I said to him, 'I'll think about it over the weekend'. So I told Tommy. He said, 'What's he offered you?' I said, 'He's offered me a bit more money.' 'We'll give you the same' he said, 'and stay here'. So I said okay. I loved Chelsea but they were in financial trouble. They were in a bit of a mess, so I wasn't that keen to go at the time. Also, I loved United."

OCTOBER

FULHAM 1-2 MANCHESTER UNITED

Stepney, Forsyth, Houston, Greenhoff, Holton, Buchan, Morgan, McIlroy, Pearson[2], McCalliog, Daly (Macari)

Blunstone was, as it turned out, in South West London for the start of October but only accompanying United in their game at Fulham, where the hosts were bullishly aware of the difficult task they faced. "United's attempt to get back to the First Division has brought the spotlight to the Second Division this season and from what we have seen the Division is standing up well to examination," the 'Cottage Comment' introduction of their match-day programme said.

Welcome to Craven Cottage

FULHAM v MANCHESTER UNITED
Football League Division Two
Saturday 5 October 1974   Kick-off 3.00 pm
Official Matchday Magazine 10p

"Obviously Tommy Docherty and his men know that promotion is by no means guaranteed for any club. That was brought home to them with a bang at Norwich last Saturday when Norwich beat the 2-0 to take away their unbeaten record. Doubtless this will make United redouble their efforts today – for not only did we beat Norwich 4-0 two weeks ago but we are one of the main challengers to the men from Old Trafford. To us United are not only a great club, whose presence in the opposite half of the field always sets the heart beating faster, they are a symbol of the standard we must reach if ambitions are to be realised. We are not afraid that our football will fall below the level necessary to beat teams like United..."

A profile on their opponents elsewhere in the programme conceded, "With Manchester United firmly at the head of the Second Division, it would take a brave man, or a fool, to bet against their going up next April." The game itself was far from a formality with Fulham proving to be the competitive opponents they had promised – United were seemingly unaffected by their defeat at Carrow Road in their confident start while their hosts gave as good as they got. On 17 minutes, the Reds got a vital grip on the points after taking the lead through the returning Stuart Pearson. McIlroy had created the goal with fantastic work in the build up and it was in fact his shot that Pearson deflected in. If that wasn't enough, there was further confusion over who the scorer was – Pearson's effort had just gone over the line but an attempted clearance in vain from a Fulham defender was intercepted by Gerry Daly anyhow, and he made sure that the ball went in by smashing it home convincingly.

As Fulham pressed hard for an equaliser in the second half, United broke away but there was more than just an element of luck in the goal that was to settle the game. The Cottagers seemingly regained control of the ball but a mix up between goalkeeper Peter Mellor and Fulham legend Alan Mullery gifted Pearson a golden opportunity to double his tally. He made no mistake. Viv Busby pulled back a late goal but it wasn't enough to prevent United – bolstered by the return of Jim Holton in defence – from leaving London with two points and a renewed belief heading into the biggest game of the season yet.

Manchester City had been League Cup winners as recently as 1970 while United had never won it; however, there was a greater significance about the forthcoming League Cup tie as it was the first since the infamous encounter the previous April and presented the Reds with an unexpected and early opportunity to exact some sort of revenge.

Manager Tommy Docherty was more interested in the occasion rather than the plot in his programme notes. "There is magic in the air tonight all right!" he proclaimed. "Old Trafford is no doubt a full house of nearly 60,000 and the atmosphere is tremendous. Doesn't it make you glad to live in Manchester and find yourself caught up in the excitement of a derby like this evening's match?... My only regret is that this is not the final of the League Cup and that we should have met so early in the competition. Only one team can go forward and that will be a loss for Manchester, the city which for me is the capital of football."

WEDNESDAY 9TH OCTOBER - LEAGUE CUP THIRD ROUND - OLD TRAFFORD (55,159)

MANCHESTER UNITED 1-0 MANCHESTER CITY

Stepney, Forsyth, Albiston, Greenhoff, Holton, Buchan, Morgan, McIlroy, Pearson, McCalliog, Daly [1+]
Sub: Macari

Blooding youngsters in English football's secondary Cup competition is part of the fabric of Manchester United but it was through necessity rather than choice that Docherty was forced to hand 17 year-old Arthur Albiston his first team debut. Stewart Houston had picked up an injury at Fulham and rather than make changes elsewhere, the manager decided to select his young compatriot. It would have perhaps made sense to move Brian Greenhoff

to left back due to his versatility, which would then have seen Lou Macari move into midfield. If such an observation seems pointless to the narrative, it is made with reference to the fact that Greenhoff would later state he played in every single position for United (including a second half in goal at Birmingham a couple of years later following an injury to Alex Stepney) except for left back. The accommodating Yorkshireman did concede he wouldn't have been comfortable there – so maybe it was something that had been discussed prior to the match.

The sides had previously met in the competition during City's

1970 success – though 'revenge' was solely about April than what was now considered ancient history. After playing 'bad cop' for most of the season, Docherty was keen to afford praise to the United support in his notes before the match. "...I also feel that the crowd situation is going to pass off a lot more quietly than some people seem to expect. I must stress that despite our fences behind each goal we have had very little trouble here at Old Trafford on the terraces... It's not for me to argue the rights and wrongs of that instruction (to install the fences), except to say that last season was rather tragic for this club. Those kids rushed on to the pitch when they realised we were going into the Second Division, and they always come on to the pitch anyway at the end of the final home match. The point I want to make is that we do not have a long history of trouble inside our ground and I see no reason why this evening's fixture will not go off just as smoothly as practically every other League game, including the many derby matches that have been played over the years between City and United."

Relegation often comes with the inevitable price of fading from the public spotlight but that couldn't be further from the truth from United, whose regeneration was capturing the imagination of supporters and also attracting much praise from a number of clubs who were getting the opportunity to play them twice when they would normally have to hope for the luck of a Cup draw. Despite the controversy that had dogged the start of the season, there was a widespread admiration for the way that United supporters had continued to back their team in numbers. The gate against City was the highest in all of English football so far that season. The fifty-five thousand in attendance were treated to a typical blood and thunder derby game – and the players were treated to an atmosphere that had been missing from Manchester derbies for a fair few years.

Ronald Crowther reported in his *Daily Mail* column that

despite the tension, "...both these Manchester sides honoured their pledge to make it the friendly derby that erased so many of the lingering memories of their bitter brawls of the past."

City came into the game in third place in Division One and full of the confidence one might expect; the Reds weathered an early storm which included a Rodney Marsh goal which was disallowed for a foul in the build up. United might have felt up against it when Pearson was forced to come off with another injury but, spurred on by a vociferous crowd, they grew into the game and began to have the better of the second half. Jim McCalliog had two great chances - one long range effort that had City stopper Keith MacRae scrambling back to save, and one from inside the area that was blocked by his own team mate, McIlroy.

It was through McCalliog that the breakthrough eventually came; his cross was handled by City defender Clarke, who flustered under pressure from Macari. Gerry Daly's record from the spot so far had been perfect and he converted in the 74th minute to give United an advantage they had just about earned.

City's exploration for an equaliser didn't present any clear cut opportunities, but they came close - Mike Summerbee was the intended recipient of a through ball that would have put him clean through with only Stepney to beat, but Albiston pulled off a miraculous sweeping tackle to intercept the pass.

United's reward for their narrow victory was another local derby at home, this time against Burnley, also of the First Division. Before that, Docherty's side had the serious business of Division Two to deal with, and a visit from eleventh placed Notts County.

SATURDAY 12TH OCTOBER - DIVISION TWO - OLD TRAFFORD (46,515)

MANCHESTER UNITED 1-0 NOTTS COUNTY

Stepney, Forsyth, Houston, Greenhoff, Holton, Buchan, Morgan, McIlroy[1], Macari, McCalliog (Young), Daly

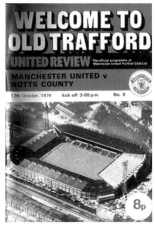

Welcoming back Houston but having to do without Pearson once more, United made tough work of overcoming a Notts County side who seemed content to have possession but never seemed to want to do anything. It was probably just as well, then, that the hosts got the decisive goal as early as the 17th minute, to avoid any late anxiety – and in doing so, managing to deflate County who had started relatively positively. Greenhoff, Morgan and Forysth were all involved in a neat build up – Gerry Daly received the ball and found McIlroy, who finished just inside the post. Journalist Bert Thorpe reported "United threatened to swamp County but (County keeper Roy) Brown saved superbly from Martin Buchan, Greenhoff and Lou Macari."

"The sparkle of last Wednesday's win over Manchester City was missing from United," continued Thorpe, "and Notts County gave the league leaders as hard a game as any other side has at Old Trafford this season."

The speed in which the fixtures came – particularly the home games – meant that it was not always possible for a new match programme to be printed referring to events in a game three days prior. In that case, it would be common for Docherty to use his notes to reflect on a game that was prior to the last one, making them seem of out of sync. This was the case in the match programme for the County game where, after praising supporters ahead of the City Cup tie, he was forced to comment on minor incidents that had made the press following the Fulham game.

"Our gates are up on last season's average and everywhere we go we seem to take such a tremendous following. The host clubs never cease to be amazed," explained Docherty. "Take our visit to Fulham last weekend. The 26,500 gate was more than three times the usual crowd at Craven Cottage this season. Because of the behaviour of the irresponsible few, the newspaper headlines are invariably based on the special police plans to control the fans and if there is any trouble you can be sure it will hit the news. But look at the other side of the coin for a moment. For every lad that causes damage, there are hundreds whose crime is nothing more than whooping up a bit of excitement, bringing life to the game and obtaining a great deal of pleasure from their total commitment to the support of Manchester United. The fact that there has to be extra police on duty is not necessarily a crime in itself. If you suddenly have a crowd treble the usual size it is one commonsense to have three times the usual number of police... I for one would rather have the problem of hooliganism than no fans! That does not mean I am complacent about the trouble it causes for other people, simply that at least it gives us something slightly easier to tackle than trying to reach out to empty spaces." There can be no doubt that if not exactly sympathising, Docherty had gone about things in an orderly fashion – firstly condemning the acts and later attempting to logically present all sides of the argument.

Elsewhere in the same programme, a feature by Tony Pullein celebrated the popularly to which Docherty had hinted. "We don't need telling that Manchester United are the most popular team in Division Two. But the enormity of our success is truly staggering," wrote Pullein. "Old Trafford crowds are 33 per cent higher than any other Second Division club and, for three of our first four away matches, we more than doubled the home club's average attendance!"

TUESDAY 15TH OCTOBER - DIVISION TWO - FRATTON PARK (25,608)

PORTSMOUTH 0-0 MANCHESTER UNITED

Stepney, Forsyth, Albiston, Greenhoff, Holton, Buchan, Morgan (McCreery), McIlroy, Macari, McCalliog, Daly

It was a case of déjà vu for all involved in the return game against Portsmouth. Another away game with a huge following – Portsmouth's biggest crowd of the season so far had been the previous Saturday, when 12,520 turned up to watch their dour goalless draw with Fulham. Clearly, United were not the only team to suffer from Pompey's spoiling tactics, but since the two met in August, manager John Mortimore had been replaced by Ian St. John.

St. John's programme notes insisted that the draw with Fulham had been a point lost instead of gained and, perhaps fuelled by his ex-Liverpool ties, he spoke rather discourteously about his latest visitors. "So tonight we are at home to high-riding Manchester United," he wrote. "For days now all I have heard people saying is that 'this is the big one'. What do they mean when they say 'this is the big one'? Listen, every match is a big one in the Football League, regardless of division. Sure, Manchester United were aristocrats in the First Division. Sure, they were among the elite in soccer's high society. That was last season... or maybe a season or two before. They are in the Second Division now and admittedly look good for promotion, but until they get back up among the big boys in the First Division they cannot be considered superstars. Don't forget Oldham Athletic were once in the First Division. No one heralded them to Fratton Park with the ballyhoo which seems to be reserved for Manchester United. I keep telling everyone that, in football, memories don't live longer than dreams. Notts County were founder members of the Football League and look at the struggle they had getting from the Fourth Division to the Second. And founder members Accrington Stanley are now not even in the League. All this adulation of Manchester United makes them walk ten-foot tall. They have an advantage over the opposition before the match even starts. They will have no advantage tonight, for my team have been told repeatedly to treat them as any other Second Division side."

For all of St. John's protestations he couldn't argue with the fact that his home crowd was more than twice as large as it would be for the rest of the season, and nobody could gloss over the non-spectacle of an event that was advertised as a football match beforehand. United were described as 'casual and over confident' in one report that opened with the statement 'Portsmouth proved what we have increasingly seen this season – that Manchester United will have to play twice as well as most teams to ensure promotion'.

Brian Greenhoff later referred to it as 'the worst game I ever played in'. "A big centre half called Eoin Hand was marking me," said Brian. "He said 'My boss must fancy you because he's told me I've got to run around with you all game!'. They played man for man on everybody and made it a complete non-entity."

Arthur Albiston was given his League debut after Houston had struggled to play with his injury against Notts County and David McCreery, who had only just turned 17, was brought on in the second half for the ineffectual Willie Morgan. Whether Morgan was frustrated with the manager or the suffocating tactics of Portsmouth, he took it out on Docherty. "We went to the Playboy club at Southsea after the game and Willie went really over the top, saying he was finished with the manager," remembered Brian. "I don't know why he was so upset – when they held up his number, we were all disappointed because it was such a poor game we all wanted to come off!" The club's newsletter made mention of McCreery's debut, saying 'many experts reckon (he) is the best prospect to come out of the Old Trafford youth ranks since George Best'.

From the ridiculous and forgettable to the sublime and the memorable – United's next game was another away game, this time at Blackpool. There were natural concerns, with both clubs having faced unfavourable press for the behaviour of their supporters – so much so that John McDermott, the Blackpool Shopkeeper's Leader, made an unsuccessful appeal to the Prime Minister Harold Wilson to have the match postponed or ban United fans from the town until the 'Illuminations' event had ended.

Blackpool manager Harry Potts used his programme notes to attempt to engineer a more positive welcome. "This is undoubtedly a day-of-days for Bloomfield Road, with those celebrated "Red Devils" – Manchester United – as Blackpool's opponents," beamed Potts in his column that was on the page opposite a competition advertisement offering two match goers a 'finger lickin' twenty two pieces (each!) of Kentucky Fried Chicken.

Elsewhere in Blackpool's entertaining publication was possibly one of the first recorded pieces of evidence of the 'WAG' culture, with a feature, 'Behind Every Man...' on Marjorie Bentley, wife of Blackpool centre half Bill.

"Majorie doesn't go out to work, though she is looking forward to getting a job when the family grow up. 'I really would like to go out to work when the children are both at school. Mind you, I'm pretty busy at home at the moment. I make most of my own clothes and the children's clothes and I also make a lot of Bill's clothes.'

"'She does, she's very good. She made these trousers I'm wearing,' Bill interrupted."

S<small>ATURDAY</small> 19<small>TH</small> O<small>CTOBER</small> - D<small>IVISION</small> T<small>WO</small> - B<small>LOOMFIELD</small> R<small>OAD</small> (22,211)

BLACKPOOL 0-3 MANCHESTER UNITED

Stepney, Forsyth[1], Houston, Greenhoff, Holton, Buchan, Morgan, McIlroy, Macari[1], McCalliog[1], Daly (McCreery)

United's dismantling of their unsuspecting hosts was ruthless. "We played like Champions that day," Brian Greenhoff later said in his autobiography. The 22,000 crowd was between 15,000 and 16,000 Red and they weren't left disappointed with a thrilling display that Tommy Docherty later described as 'our best away performance of the season'. "We did not have a bad player in the side," he said. "Everyone excelled to make it a tremendous all-round team performance. We were strong at

the back with everyone going forward and carrying a marvellous exhibition of attacking football to its logical conclusion with three goals."

Those goals were scored by Alex Forsyth with a stunning, powerful free kick, Lou Macari after good work by Jim McCalliog, who then scored himself with an impudent chip to put the perfect seal on the result. "A shower of rain greeted the players when the teams came out, but it did not dampen the tremendous roar that greeted the Reds from their following of over 15,000 fans," said one report. The 1-0 half time scoreline flattered the hosts who had escaped being further behind thanks to an offside flag that ruled out a goal from Sammy McIlroy.

There was the hint of trouble when police were forced to accost a pitch invader from the away end during the interval, which had also seen Sir Matt Busby take to the field to award a Cup to United fans who had won the "It's a Knockout!" competition before the game.

David Meek later proclaimed the 'record breaking progress' made by United in the Division, tipping them to beat the points record set by Middlesbrough in '73/74. "It is perhaps asking a lot to expect United to maintain their present progress, but after the high point of their 3-0 win at Blackpool, nothing would seem impossible," wrote Meek. "United overwhelmed the opposition at Bloomfield Road in all departments. It started at the back with solid defence that was turned quickly into attack through full backs Alex Forsyth and Stewart Houston. Indeed it was Forsyth who opened the scoring when he shot low and hard through the defensive wall to score with a free kick just inside the post. The mid-field players took a firm grip on the match with Lou Macari and Jim McCalliog adding the other goals. Macari and Sammy McIlroy were particularly impressive with their movement off the ball, constantly switching position and bewildering the Bloomfield Road defence."

Indeed, Blackpool's players were effusive in their praise afterwards. "They were so good that they were taking the mickey out of us for the last twenty minutes," said George Wood. Dave Hatton agreed, saying they felt 'paralysed'.

The Blackpool game was the scene for Martin Buchan's fondest memory of the entire campaign. "We were playing at Blackpool and there was a ball played through the inside right channel and coming towards me," he recounts. "I was stood just inside our half and there was a Blackpool player running towards me, charging towards me. Without thinking, all of a sudden, I feinted moving forward, and flicked the ball with my right heel behind my left foot towards Stewart Houston. After moving the ball on, Stewart turned back towards me and bowed. It was like something you'd expect a Brazilian to do. I thought I was going to get hammered as the ball was coming at quite a pace. It summed up how we all played on the day as that was a memorable game for us. I remember

The Red Army take over Blackpool

Jim McCalliog scoring with a great chip. I don't remember results and scorelines like fans do but I remember incidents in games like those."

United, as a whole, were clearly in the groove and the comprehensive win moved them four points ahead at the top of the table, and just to underline their impressive start, they were also the top scorers in the league. The result was their fifth away win in just eight away league games, further evidence of their ambition to win every time they played – a points haul of 23 from a possible 28 had put the Reds in a commanding position. A third of the way through the season and Docherty had got his team exactly where he wanted them. With the winter approaching, there was the suggestion that United's brand of football might not survive in the harsh conditions and the unforgiving playing surfaces that clubs without the resources of the top league had to use. Docherty refuted this, saying, "I just don't see heavier grounds as a danger. We play it short and we play it long all the time anyway... Jim Holton, Stewart Houston and Alex Forysth will probably play better on heavy grounds and Martin Buchan is playing brilliantly on any surface. Brian Greenhoff is a strong player and so also is Stuart Pearson."

If he was confident in his team's ability, the manager was quick to dismiss any thoughts of complacency. "There is a long way to go yet of course and you won't find me counting our chickens until April," the manager wrote in his pre-match notes ahead of the next game, against Southampton. "At the same time it would be churlish not to express appreciation and satisfaction with what the players have achieved in their first 14 games in the Second Division. The lads have worked hard and they have worked well. I don't think we have been particularly lucky; at the same time we have not had much desperate bad luck either."

Indeed, if there had been an on-pitch disappointment so far, it was the failure to get Stuart Pearson in a run of games. The forward was back in contention to play against the Saints but, due to the previous performance, Docherty had reservations about changing the team. "The niggling injury to Stuart Pearson has been a nuisance, but fortunately we have had the reserve strength to cover his absence and Lou Macari has played with tremendous spirit in his place," wrote Docherty. "Lou did not find it easy to settle into English League football, and yet this season when he has had the rather unsettling experience of being in and out of the team, his attitude has been great and he has struck his best form since I signed him. I was left with a very difficult situation when I selected the side to play Southampton this afternoon with Stuart Pearson available again after his injury and the whole team playing so well in the game at Blackpool last weekend. It is the kind of problem all managers like to be faced with of course, but it was nevertheless very tough to be fair to everyone. The only thing I know at this stage writing this article is that whatever my decision I can count on it being accepted by the players involved in the right spirit from the club point of view."

<small>SATURDAY 26TH OCTOBER - DIVISION TWO - OLD TRAFFORD</small> (48,724)

MANCHESTER UNITED 1-0 SOUTHAMPTON

Stepney, Forsyth, Houston, Greenhoff, Holton, Buchan, Morgan (Pearson[1]), McIlroy, Macari, McCalliog, Daly

In addition to the above, Docherty had also written "...without the right spirit and attitude in the dressing room a club is struggling. Happily we still managed to create the correct feeling and approach when things were going against us during relegation and I am glad to say that we still have a happy atmosphere during this much happier season with so much going well for us," in his notes. The words could scarcely have been more ironic, as it would be fair to say that if there was ever

a day of internal discontent at Old Trafford in this season, it was on Saturday 26th October (and there were a few to choose from).

Docherty had decided against starting with Pearson, sensibly keeping faith with a winning team, but United lacked the cutting edge and swagger that had illuminated their performance against Blackpool. As supporters became frustrated, they began to chant for Pearson to be brought on – but when Willie Morgan was the man brought off with twenty five minutes left, there were mixed emotions in the crowd. Morgan was furious. "I was so sick that I got changed and went straight home without waiting for the end," he later said. This episode followed the Portsmouth game as examples of the beginning of the fallout between Docherty and

Morgan in a month where Docherty also alleged to the board that Morgan had requested a transfer – a request the manager had refused. It later transpired that Morgan had made no such request, but it was not the last time that the two would fall out this season.

Morgan felt that Docherty's increasingly regular substitutions of him were done to purposely humiliate him and while it is difficult to make an impartial, objective comment on that, one must point to the fact that even the greatest players are brought off, and in this event at least, the manager made the right call, because Pearson scored with around twelve minutes remaining with the glancing header which bore the hallmark of a true poacher.

Pearson's very presence in the team also caused Macari to voice his disillusion following United's narrow 1-0 win. "I'm not being conceited, but I believe that I am playing well enough to be in the first team whether Pearson is fit or not. If I find that I am still considered only for the first team as stand-in for him then I shall have to have a think about my situation," the Scot said, before then suggesting that all was not well in his own relationship with the manager. "Let's face it, I wasn't left out of the first team in the first place this season because of my ability on the field. It was something behind the scenes, as the saying goes, and I don't want to talk about it," said Macari. He was in the midst of being converted into a midfielder and now, with the benefit of hindsight – he seemed at ease with the move. "I played a season up front in England and I could handle it because I'd done so for Celtic, and scored goals too," he said. "In Scotland, though, there were a lot of small players, and in England, there weren't many small centre forwards – but there were many big centre halves! You were more easily marked as a result. Being someone who liked to get around the pitch, I felt that moving back into midfield was the best thing for me, and it showed in my performances. Probably the worst season I had in terms of goalscoring was the year I played up front!

As soon as I went into midfield I was hitting double figures most season. I don't think that my positional move had anything to do with Stuart Pearson or anyone we brought in for that matter, it was just where I was playing best, and I think that had long been on the Doc's mind too."

Macari may have had more of a reason to feel disgruntled than Morgan as his on and off first team position meant he wasn't selected for Scotland's International friendly with East Germany. In his 'Club Topics' column in the programme for the game against Oxford United, David Meek spoke glowingly of United's international contingent. "Manchester United were back in the international swim in a big way this week," he wrote. "They provided nine players for four different countries. Willie Morgan, Martin Buchan, Jim Holton and Alex Forsyth were in Glasgow for Scotland's friendly against East Germany. Incidentally I wonder why Scotland did not go the whole way and pick Stewart Houston as well. That way they could have played their back-four defence as a unit from one club, a great stride towards creating an understanding in a side... The Republic of Ireland came next by asking for three United men – Gerry Daly, Mick Martin and Paddy Roche. They were wanted for their Nations Cup match against Russia in Dublin. Sammy McIlroy went to Stockholm for Northern Ireland's match against Sweden and Brian Greenhoff was called up for the England Under-23 match against Czechoslovakia in London. No wonder with his senior playing staff so widely dispersed that manager Tommy Docherty called for an immediate return of his players after their international fixtures."

If there was any dissension in the ranks then Docherty was doing his best to concentrate on the external opposition that was becoming an increasingly familiar sight – teams going to Old Trafford with no intention of going for the win. "It takes many qualities to make up a successful football team," wrote Docherty ahead of welcoming Oxford United to Manchester in programme notes that gave more away than usual. "There are the obvious ones like the skill factor, fitness, determination and spirit. I think Manchester United have shown all these characteristics... But now our position calls for something else, yet another quality which is not so obvious but which will be necessary for us to hold our lead through the remainder of the season. The team have got to be patient. Now patience is not the kind of virtue one normally associated with the hurly-burly of soccer, but I believe it is important for a team at the top. We have got to show patience when we are playing at home. Having established ourselves in the lead, a good number of teams are going to come to Old Trafford with the idea of playing defensively. This is going to frustrate us and in that mood we shall have to be careful. It is only too easy for a frustrated team to get careless in defence and then get so desperate to score against a packed defence that the attack loses its rhythm and poise. Players can start lobbing the ball into a crowded penalty area and forget the build up that draws players out of position. A team can lose the whole pattern purely through the frustration of playing against opponents who come content to settle for a draw.

"Southampton were typical of this last approach last weekend. They came for a point and resorted to quite tough tactics in their tackling to get it. It was a highly frustrating situation for us. But we showed commendable patience and did not lose either our control or the pattern of our player. It brought us a late goal from Stuart Pearson and full points. But the match could so easily have ended in a draw. I have in fact told the players that they have got to show this kind of patience and even extend it to drawing on our own ground. I can forsee several games when we shall have to be content with a point at home, not the kind of result I would like ideally in front of our tremendous support, but nevertheless inevitable against teams who won't open up the play.

"I reckon it could now become easier for us to win when we play away. The ease of our victory at Blackpool followed by the frustrations against Southampton illustrate what I am saying. Patience and restraint saw us through against Southampton and if we can maintain this patient quality it might well thwart the frustrating teams. This is the theme I have been trying to get over to the lads this week as we prepared for the visit of Oxford United. I would like you supporters to appreciate the situations as well, because I am the first to admit that the kind of game you saw last week does not make very good entertainment. This was sad with an attendance of 48,724, our biggest League crowd of the season so far. So I hope you fans will also be patient and bear with the problems which I hope we shall still beat... provided we show the necessary patience!"

It could be said that Docherty genuinely believed that the eye operation Willie Morgan had in the summer had a profound impact on the winger's sensational dribbling ability and creativity. The one thing that is true above all else was that the manager of Manchester United was primarily required to win football matches and pick the team he felt was most capable of achieving this result. Maybe with the above words about patience in his mind, Docherty made a stunning call by dropping Morgan and selecting Macari in his place. Once more, the manager's tough choice was vindicated by the result.

NOVEMBER

MANCHESTER UNITED 4-0 OXFORD UNITED

Stepney, Forsyth, Houston, Greenhoff (Morgan), Sidebottom, Buchan, Macari[1], McIlroy, Pearson[3], McCalliog, Daly

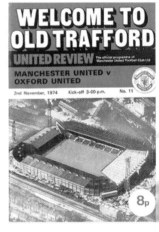

"We thought we would be okay if we could get over the first twenty minutes," Oxford manager Gerry Summers said after the match. "But we didn't, and United punished us for some bad defensive play." The visitor's resistance, in fact, lasted just eight minutes. There are numerous qualities required in order to pull off a game plan where your sole aim is to nullify the opposition; among them, the patience which Docherty spoke so frequently of in his own notes, discipline, and chiefly – ability. Football supporters love a David versus Goliath story but the very reason those stories are so romantic is because, more often than not, the Goliath slays the David, and that was the case in this early November encounter.

It was Stuart Pearson who was grabbing the headlines with this eye-catching performance which immediately had some suggesting 'Pancho' could be in line for an England call-up. It was Pearson who broke the deadlock in similar fashion to how he grabbed the opener against Fulham; diverting an already goal-bound header from Gerry Daly into the Oxford goal. On 24 minutes, another similar goal was scored – this time, the 'victim' of that goal at Craven Cottage, McIlroy, lost out on a goal again as

Pearson nods home the first against Oxford

Macari stole in to make a telling deflection and double United's advantage.

Only 32 minutes were on the clock by the time the hosts made it three - Pearson grabbing his second with another well timed and well placed header. On the stroke of half time he was handed his hat-trick goal on a plate thanks to the invention of McIlroy. The scoring was done but the entertainment wasn't, with the second Club newsletter of the season reporting that at full time, 'United left the field to a rapturous ovation for the second time in one match'.

Pearson was understandably elated afterwards. "This is easily the best Second Division side I have played in - a class above anything else... it's tremendous playing in front of this crowd. How can any player fail to be motivated by it?" he said.

Today, Arnie Sidebottom says he feels a little sympathy for players who felt anything but motivated. "I remember teams coming to Old Trafford in front of the huge crowds and they were just absolutely petrified," he says. "It was like nothing they'd seen. Against Oxford United it seemed like we were 4-0 up inside ten minutes. It was a totally different world for some of those clubs."

The match programme featured an extract from Fulham's own match publication dated 19th October, praising the behaviour of recent visiting fans from the United's of Manchester and West Ham. "For both matches we would like to thank home and visiting supporters, the police, our staff and the players for two tremendous trouble free matches which went far to prove that soccer is not the dead duck the moaners would have us believe," read the extract, followed by a comment by United themselves. "We are pleased to print this tribute to our players and supporters from Fulham FC and would like it to be known that the Police view after the match at Blackpool was 'that the trouble was no worse than they experience any weekend while the illuminations are on.'"

In the Oxford programme there was also an interesting letter sent in from author John Bill, who spoke of a book "Kings of English Football" that featured an introduction from Sir Matt Busby. Bond was responding to a special feature in the *Manchester Evening News* on the recent Cup derby and sent in a list of noteworthy accolades and achievements by the club to that point, including player achievements and attendance awards.

1946-74 - 28 SEASONS

Higher League Position United : 22 times City : 6 times
First Division Points: United : 1378 City : 939
First Division Championships: United : 5 City : 1
Runners-Up: United : 7 City : 0
European CupWinners : United 1 City 0
FA Youth Cup Winners: United : 6 City : 0

In their 29 seasons of continuous membership of the First Division to the end of last season Manchester United obtained more points (1416) than any other club, won most matches (552) scored most goals (2252) won most FA Cup ties (67), fielded most International players (48), with most International appearances (530), won most championships, most times runners–up, most times in top four (15), played in most FA Cup Finals and semi-finals, also quarter-finals (14). Unequalled in European Cup, FA Charity Shield and FA Youth Cup...

Other records

★ Only club to defeat six First Division opponents in winning the FA Cup (1948), Duncan Edwards youngest player ever to play for England. Only club to have three players (Bobby Charlton, Denis Law, George Best) winning one or both honours, Player of the Year and European Player of the Year...

★ Highest average attendance for a season 57,696 in 1967/68. Sir Matt Busby, the only manager in the history of the League to manage five Championship teams.

★ The only club in the First Division which can possibly overhaul United's total of 1378 points in post-war matches during the present season is Arsenal, requiring a minimum of 60 at the beginning of the season. Having obtained seven points from their first 12 matches they still need 53 from their remaining 30 games.

★ In spite of all we hear, Liverpool with 986 points, Spurs with 1158 and Leeds with 756 and all the others are trailing well behind the Reds."

Who said statistics were an invention of the 21st century?! Incidentally, Bill explained that the publishers of the book had gone bankrupt and that he hoped it would be republished in 1975.

If the book eventually did get published, it is rarer than hen's teeth.

United's next 90 minutes took place in the Emerald Isle in a friendly match against Shelbourne which had been arranged due to the transfer of Paddy Roche the previous year.

WEDNESDAY 6TH NOVEMBER - FRIENDLY - DALYMOUNT PARK (20,000)

SHELBOURNE 1-1 MANCHESTER UNITED

Roche, Forsyth, Houston, Greenhoff, Sidebottom, Buchan, Macari, McCreery, Pearson, McCalliog, Daly[1]
Sub: Morgan, Young, Martin

Gerry Doyle extended a cordial welcome to his team's glamour opponents in the eight page match programme. "At last, the Reds of Manchester meet the Reds of Dublin," he wrote. "This is something we in Shelbourne have looked forward to ever since Tony Dunne joined United after playing in our Cup-winning side of 1960... may we say good luck, Doc and may we all rejoice with you and your boys when you return to your rightful place in the First Division."

United took over a strong side but apparently the names weren't too familiar to the programme editor, with 'Forsythe', 'Houstan', 'McElroy' and a 'T. Sidebottom' apparently taking their place in the visiting line-up.

The Reds had played against Shamrock Rovers at the same venue in October 1973 and that game had to be abandoned with around ten minutes left due to a pitch invasion. After Shelbourne took an early lead, the second half saw two incidents (pitch invasions and missiles being thrown) that caused delays of around a quarter of an hour. As the official newsletter reported, "With only 2 minutes to go in this friendly match... Gerry Daly spared United a lot of embarrassment by snatching a late equaliser." David Meek later wrote in his programme column, "...the Reds had not bargained for their tremendous popularity in Ireland bringing the chaos and stoppage that held up the game..."

The sense that this was a game United could have done without was confirmed when Jim McCalliog was carried off injured – making him a significant doubt for the weekend's League game at Bristol City.

SATURDAY 9TH NOVEMBER - DIVISION TWO - ASHTON GATE (28,104)

BRISTOL CITY 1-0 MANCHESTER UNITED

Stepney, Forsyth, Houston, Greenhoff, Sidebottom, Buchan, Macari, McIlroy, Pearson, McCalliog, Daly (Graham)

Home manager Alan Dicks surprisingly made no mention whatsoever of his team's opponents for what was undoubtedly their biggest game of the season. Although City supporters may contend that and say their local rivalry with Rovers was a bigger game, there could be no arguing about United's stature. City had welcomed Liverpool for a League Cup tie earlier in the season and attracted a crowd of 25,573. When United came to town, almost two and a half thousand more supporters squeezed into Ashton Gate.

Such an attendance was a much welcome boost for Dicks whose main concern was the financial situation at the club; programme columnist Tony Rance echoed these thoughts on page nine. "...Today is our first sponsored match at Bristol City and with such illustrious visitors as Manchester United the ingredients all seem set for a memorable occasion. Why do we need sponsored matches? The short answer to this question is – MONEY."

The romance of a performance against United was almost rendered a mere subplot for a club whose previous biggest gate of the League season was 15,708 against Southampton but whose regular attendance was around the 11,000 mark. Ironic, then, that the team pulled off a memorable result on the day. City were boosted by the confidence which had come with three consecutive wins and clean sheets that had also seen them climb up to fifth position in the League.

United – with the recovered McCalliog – threatened early on but on the half hour John Emanuel scored for Dicks' men to end the visitors' own run of six consecutive clean sheets. Docherty's response was to bring on the ostracised George Graham, who'd played with the reserves all season, for Daly at half time. It wasn't enough to invigorate a subdued Reds side who simply couldn't get going in the second half – it was 'one of those days' for United, who slumped to their second defeat of the season, though with a five point advantage heading into the game, it was one they could afford.

Even that consolation was not enough to prevent a group of angry United supporters from going on the rampage in Bristol afterwards. 'City in terror as Soccer fans go wild' read one headline of an article that claimed 'They smashed windows of houses, overturned cars and demolished garden fences... Mobs of United fans, waving their red and white scarves, charged along roads leading from the ground. Within minutes, the switchboard at the city's police headquarters was jammed with calls from householders complaining that fans were hurling stones through windows and at cars'.

Docherty's programme notes for the following league game concentrated on the performance – or lack of it – rather than the violence which had followed. "...We must be on our guard against these promotion rivals and we must certainly play a good deal better than we did at Bristol. We just never got going. Passing the ball accurately is usually one of our strong points but at Ashton Gate it was awful. We have a catchphrase in training to encourage the players to do the safe, simple thing; pass to the nearest red shirt, we say. Perhaps that was our mistake because at Bristol we had to change to an all-white strip with the home team playing in red. And we certainly gave those red shirts a generous share of our passes," wrote the Doc in trademark wisecracking style. "More seriously, we have no excuses. We just didn't play well and Bristol took advantage."

One slightly less controversial but nonetheless interesting side note to take from the Bristol game was alluded to in Docherty's comments. United were in the final season of wearing Umbro manufactured strips ahead of their switch to Admiral in 1975. Strangely, United changed both their home and away strips after the Bristol game. They had worn a red shirt with a white collar and cuffs since 1971, with the crest on since 1972, while their away strip from the previous season had been all white (with a third strip of yellow and blue which was rarely worn).

For the next game, against Burnley in the League Cup, United wore a new home strip that now had a button up front instead of the white chest piece; their new away strip was a white variant of the home. A new third strip – blue shirt and white shorts – was worn for the Walsall Cup tie in January 1975 as well as the Southampton away game in April. While no significant mention was made of the change in the club's publications, it did at least warrant a mention in the club's official newsletter's review of the Burnley tie.

Wednesday 13th November - League Cup fourth round
Old Trafford (46,269)

MANCHESTER UNITED 3-2 BURNLEY

Stepney, Forsyth, Houston, Greenhoff (Morgan[1]), Sidebottom, Buchan, Macari[2], McIlroy, Pearson, McCalliog, Daly

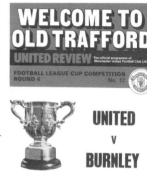

"United playing in new-style shirts (white open-neck collar without the small triangle of white), won through to the League Cup 5th Round by virtue of this 3-2 victory over Burnley at Old Trafford. But it was not until 3 minutes from the end that the tie was decided, with Lou Macari getting his second goal of the match... The Reds first goal, which was sandwiched by Burnley's two, was a beautiful move. Alex Forsyth, who had received a short ball from Willie Morgan, who had come on for the injured Brian Greenhoff, sent a wonderful pass to Lou Macari, who sent a first time shot past the helpless Stevenson in the Burnley goal. Starting the second period a goal down, the Reds took only 5 minutes to level the scores. Willie Morgan being the scorer, his first since the opening day of the season. Willie received the ball on the edge of the penalty area, after Colin Waldron had headed out a Jim McCalliog corner, and without hesitating he floated the ball over a mass of players and into the net. In the 87th minute Lou Macari hit the winner after striking the post with his first shot," described the newsletter.

A footnote also explained that the Reds' had struck an incredible 30 shots on target against their First Division opponents - with every outfield player having had an effort, a 'record in TV sport so far this season'.

United's resilience - and indeed, dominance - would not have come as a surprise to Tommy Docherty, who had insisted on it in his pre-match notes. "It's quite true that I want a make or break run in the League Cup," he admitted. "But don't get the idea that this will mean a half-hearted attempt in this cup competition. Quite the contrary; I have told the boys that I want them to avoid a draw by winning, and even if they are behind they must not think that I am not interested in an equaliser... There is also the bonus of a possible entry into Europe of course. That is a very attractive prize for a club like Manchester United who blazed the trail for English football on the Continent and helped build an interest that is now taken for granted."

While United's stature meant that the result could barely be described as an upset, it is worth putting the win into context. Burnley were 13th in the First Division but had won at Highbury, White Hart Lane and Anfield before making the short journey to Old Trafford. Manager Jimmy Adamson had claimed before the game, "We are a bit more relaxed away from home. We tend to push the ball about with a bit more confidence and crispness; and after what we did at Liverpool we don't fear a big atmosphere or opponents with a high reputation."

"The reluctant League Cup heroes of Manchester United stormed into the quarter-finals last night with a blistering finish that was far too hot for First Division Burnley," wrote the *Daily Mail*.

If 'reluctant' was a bit of an overstatement, then Docherty was at least forthright in his programme notes for the next game, a League match with fifth-placed Aston Villa (who had switched places with Bristol City as a consequence of each clubs' previous result). "Regardless of the outcome of the League Cup tie, this afternoon is the important match for us. I want to see us put the Bristol beating behind us and dismiss it as an isolated bad day," wrote the manager. While there was absolutely no danger that

Docherty would be relieved of his duties, David Meek reminisced about the last time United faced Aston Villa, and that Villa's unlikely League Cup triumph as a Third Division side had cost Wilf McGuinness his job.

With Jim Holton still sidelined with injury and Brian Greenhoff not deemed fit enough to start, Docherty was left with no option but to recall Willie Morgan to the starting eleven after his goalscoring exploits in midweek.

SATURDAY 16TH NOVEMBER - DIVISION TWO - OLD TRAFFORD (55,615)

MANCHESTER UNITED 2-1 ASTON VILLA

Stepney, Forsyth, Houston, Macari, Sidebottom, Buchan, Morgan McIlroy, Pearson (Greenhoff), McCalliog, Daly[2+]

If Docherty was hoping for a response the likes of which he saw in the Fulham game, he was let down – it took a long time for his team to get going, even after Villa took an early lead on 12 minutes. Two clichés in football are that you need luck and you make your own luck as well. Inspired by Lou Macari, the Reds eventually dragged themselves back into contention but required a huge slice of fortune. "The honesty of Villa goalkeeper Jimmy Cumbes got the better of his loyalty to a team that even the Stretford End must have pitied," reported *The Sun*. "No one was better placed to judge whether Manchester United were entitled to the 68th penalty that rescued them. Without his evidence I, for one, would still be inclined to believe full back John Robson's claim that he had chested rather than handled that innocuous looking cross. 'But the ball bounced from his chest on to his hand – and no matter how unlucky you consider him, it was a penalty,' admitted Cumbes."

Gerry Daly stepped up to convert his seventh penalty of the

season and thirteen minutes later Daly was on hand to convert the rebound of a saved Stewart Houston strike and put United in front. They held on for the win but *The Sun* were unconvinced. "…The euphoria of the last 22 minutes must not be allowed to obscure the unpleasant truth of the previous 68… a United defence with the best record in the country was ravaged."

Though the Reds had played a game more than their nearest rivals, the victory now extended their lead at the top of the league to six points. The only drawback was that Stuart Pearson was forced to come off with an injury that would keep him out of the League game with his former club, Hull City. Tigers manager John Kaye was keen to welcome a number of the visitors who had previously been at Boothferry Park. "Today we welcome Manchester United and especially their Manager Tommy Docherty, Tommy Cavanagh and Stuart Pearson, all of whom have had some connection with Hull City," Kaye wrote in his programme introduction. "It is always nice to renew old acquaintances and especially so today. Mind you, once we go out on the pitch we shall of course be on opposite sides, and there will be no quarter given, nor asked."

SATURDAY 23RD NOVEMBER - DIVISION TWO - BOOTHFERRY PARK (23,287)

HULL CITY 2-0 MANCHESTER UNITED

Stepney, Forsyth, Houston, Macari, Holton, Buchan, Morgan, McIlroy, Greenhoff, McCalliog, Daly

Hull's previous home gate was 7,571 against Fulham. More than three times that amount were at Boothferry Park for the visit of Manchester United to witness what Tommy Docherty later described as 'the most brutal game I've seen for five years'. His immediate post-match reaction was similarly scathing towards his former club. "I would very much like to see Hull in the First Division because they were very good to me when I was here, but my honest opinion is they won't make it. If they go on playing like this they won't have enough players left to raise a team by the end of the season. They'll have appointments at Lancaster Gate every week," he barked. "Obviously I am a little bit biased but there was some diabolical tackling… the referee never had control." Kaye had complaints of his own. "I'll agree with him that it was a keenly fought game but at least we were going for the ball," he insisted. "Willie Morgan did not do that and you should see Jimmy McGill's shin. His leg could have been broken." Morgan was not booked – four home players were, however, prompting Docherty to say, "If Hull come to Old Trafford in February and play like that there will be sendings offs as well as bookings."

Malcolm Lord's first half goal was added to by Ken Wagstaff's strike five minutes from the end to give the vicious 'Tigers' what looked like a comprehensive victory although they were under the cosh for most of the game. Two key moments in the first half – future United goalkeeper Jeff Wealand's remarkable save from Brian Greenhoff, and Alex Forsyth's untimely deflection of Lord's effort to steer it past Stepney – went against the Reds, who Docherty insisted had not disappointed him. "We played some fine football without the finish… To be honest, we were in a different class as a scientific footballing side," lamented the United manager.

Tension on the pitch was all the excuse supporters needed to cause some trouble off of it – though only 'minor' damage was caused in Hull city centre, nearly seventy supporters were ejected from the ground and twelve were arrested – two suffered suspected broken legs.

Ahead of United's following game, Docherty was boosted by the return of Stuart Pearson and Jim Holton, and also bolstered the squad with the signing of Ron Davies – the 32 year old

Portsmouth centre-forward moved to Old Trafford in exchange for George Graham. Davies could not contain his delight. "Every time I came to Old Trafford with Southampton, I said to myself: if only I could play here every other week," he admitted. "I had been seriously considering drifting off to South Africa. This move is absolutely fantastic. I'm now involved in big things with the greatest club in football. This is like a blood transfusion to me. It isn't often that a player gets such an opportunity so late in life." Davies - a Welsh international - could hardly be blamed for his excitement. He had of course got form at Old Trafford, scoring four times there in 1969 for Southampton. He was described by Cliff Butler in Bill Foulkes' autobiography as 'one of the best strikers of his generation'. Having moved to Portsmouth in 1973, he must have thought his chance at the top had gone.

The signing of Davies was made with the injury concerns over Pearson in mind. Brian Greenhoff had again shown his versatility by coming on for Pearson up front in the win over Villa and wore the number nine shirt at Hull. As admirably as Greenhoff had applied himself, the team was missing his influence further back and so when Portsmouth got in touch to enquire about the possibility of signing Graham on loan, Docherty responded that they could make it permanent if Davies came to Old Trafford.

In the match programme prior to the following game against Sunderland, David Meek wrote that 'Manchester United fans have had their fingers crossed all week for Stuart Pearson'. The North East club were second in the table and United had the opportunity to re-establish a huge six-point gap - and Tommy Docherty was keen to do so in style. "One thing I promise you... Manchester United will make their promotion bid playing football," he declared in his column. "I am prompted to say this after the disappointment of our defeat at Hull. I felt our opponents overstepped the mark with their aggression... I know that a great many of our supporters were disappointed at the result and perhaps worried that we should have lost two away matches on the trot. So it is the time to point out that I don't see the defeat as any slackening in our own team. In fact I thought we played some brilliant football. We enjoyed most of the play and while it would be fair to criticise the finishing I was completely satisfied with the manner and style of play which in the long term is the most important thing.

"It is the most important thing because it means that overall, if your standard of football is right, then you will win matches… it is football all the way for us. It will be the theme of the match this afternoon and I take great pleasure in welcoming Sunderland to Old Trafford for what I am confident will be a match in keeping with a contest between the two top teams of the division."

SATURDAY 30TH NOVEMBER - DIVISION TWO - OLD TRAFFORD (60,585)

MANCHESTER UNITED 3-2 SUNDERLAND

Stepney, Forsyth, Houston, Greenhoff (Davies), Holton, Buchan, Morgan[1], McIlroy[1], Pearson[1], Macari, Daly

Galvanised by their manager's confidence and a crowd which was the biggest in any League match in England all season, Manchester United put on a display so thrilling that it was featured on 'Match of the Day' – the BBC flagship soccer show that even then was usually solely the exclusive property of the First Division fixtures. "There isn't a superlative in the dictionary fit to describe this game adequately, so I've coined one of our own – magnifantabulous!" wrote one reporter. "This one will have Jimmy Hill purring like a kitten," remarked the proud Tommy Docherty of his team's performance.

Opposing manager Bob Stokoe wasn't quite as satisfied with

Pearson scores against Sunderland in one of the matches of the season

the game, saying, "The whole thing has been turned into 'Referee of the Day'," after a decision by the referee Gordon Hill (no, not that one!) to ignore his linesman's flag and allow Willie Morgan's equaliser to stand with the game firmly poised in the visitors' favour. Stokoe's annoyance couldn't undermine his own team's fantastic contribution to a spectacle which was brought to life in the 11th minute by the fit Pearson. Indeed, the forward looked positively sprightly as he danced around a tackle and smartly finished with his trusted left foot from twenty yards to send the home crowd crazy. Where other teams have wilted under similar pressure, the visitors showed fine resolve to level immediately - attacking straight from kick-off, Kerr won a challenge with Houston on the edge of the area and drilled a slide rule pass across goal. Sunderland number eight Billy Hughes was on hand to convert with less than twenty seconds of play between the goals.

The blue touch paper was lit and Sunderland scored another within two minutes of getting level - Bryan 'Pop' Robson and Hughes worked perfectly in tandem (a phrase that may well have been uttered many times at Old Trafford a decade later!) down the right hand side of United's defence to fashion an opportunity which the latter lashed beyond Stepney. Hughes was desperately close to a hat-trick in the first half but his volley from 18 yards was dealt with by Stepney - and then the tricky midfielder almost returned the compliment to his team-mate Robson, who latched on to a through ball, beating the offside trip but not Stepney, whose smothering of the ball kept United in a game when they were on the ropes.

Half time came at the perfect time for the Reds, who regrouped and equalised shortly after the break - Pearson beat his marker and whipped in a terrific left foot cross, which Morgan converted at the far post. The referee consulted with his linesman, who had raised his flag due to McIlroy being in an offside position - but decided the Northern Irishman was not interfering with play, much to the anger of the travelling team. With the momentum, Docherty decided to throw Davies into the action in place of Greenhoff.

Davies was instantly involved in the action - his cross field pass found Forsyth, who in turn played it to Daly. Daly's cross was met first time by McIlroy, who made no mistake from inside the area to give the Reds the lead for the second time in the game. It was a lead that they wouldn't relinquish. United had fallen behind to two goals in a matter of seconds and had responded with a quick fire double of their own, though the Morgan and McIlroy goals were six minutes apart.

For McIlroy, the winner brought immense personal satisfaction. "There were only really Villa and Sunderland who came and had a real go," he says. "They had good teams, a great away support, they were games we played in thinking it might finish 5-4. The atmosphere against Sunderland was incredible - the Stretford End was so loud. They came out flying and got in front, but we managed to turn it around. I got the winner in a 3-2 win... it was a hell of a game. I'll never forget it. It was under the lights in the second half because it was winter and everything about it was electrifying. We were so pumped up we didn't want the game to stop. They were a decent side and I think they were overwhelmed by the noise – I think it was that which got us the result that day. To score that day was incredible, one of the favourite goals of my career... not so much because of the execution or the finish, but the feeling of scoring it and the atmosphere and noise that followed. Sometimes in football the emotion and occasion is what you remember as much as how good a goal is."

Aside from the obvious boost that United received from winning such a fantastic game against their closest rivals in the Division, it was the third game in a row that the Reds had recovered from a setback in a home game to get a win. To make it the perfect day and make it a great end to the month, despite the crowd being as big as it had been anywhere in England all season, there were no arrests made.

DECEMBER

FOLLOWING THE WIN over Sunderland, everything seemed perfectly set up for United to take their good form into their League Cup Quarter Final clash at First Division Middlesbrough. Coached by Jack Charlton, Boro' were mid-table in the top flight, having lost only twice at home all season (and only four points from the top). Tellingly, though, their last home win had been in the League Cup third round almost two months earlier.

Charlton extended a few words of advice to United fans in his notes : "A word to the young Supporters of United – you have a great team with great traditions, why not make them feel as proud as you are of them. I am sure you can if you try."

WEDNESDAY 4TH DECEMBER - LEAGUE CUP - QUARTER-FINAL
AYRESOME PARK (36,005)

MIDDLESBROUGH 0-0 MANCHESTER UNITED

Stepney, Forsyth, Houston, Greenhoff, Holton, Buchan, Morgan, McIlroy, Pearson, Macari, Daly - Sub : Young

The approximate 5,000 travelling supporters were given the rare treat of getting behind an unchanged side, even if a game with Middlesbrough was something they'd seen all too often recently, having played them eight times in the previous five years in Cup games (including replays).

With that in mind, one might have assumed that both sets of players would be eager to ensure another wasn't added to the list, but despite United's positive start, the hosts quickly got a stranglehold on the match and stifled anything Docherty's men could muster. Perhaps sensing that their best chance of progression would be to win the tie at home rather than take it to a replay, Middlesbrough became more adventurous towards the end of the game. Alex Stepney had to be at his best to keep a clean sheet –

afterwards, Docherty answered questions of praise for his keeper with a stern "That's what he's paid for!" Later, Willie Morgan would suggest that the less than complimentary assessment was because Stepney was not exactly one of the Doc's 'favourites'.

Considering the dullness of the Cup tie, the most interesting snippet to take from the game probably came from Charlton's pre-game notes, where he attempted to confront some controversy that surrounded the decision to loan striker Eric McCordie to Sheffield Wednesday. "Eric was playing in the North Midland league, we felt it would do him good to sample a more competitive brand of football," protested the World Cup winner. "We offered him to Sheffield Wednesday because we knew he would do them some good. The object has been achieved, Eric has scored 6 goals in 6 matches... he will be returning to Ayresome Park (after his loan spell) and I am sure (he will) be better mentally and physically for his spell in the 2nd Division." McCordie was, of course, a United player of the past - and was to make his mark in their immediate future.

SATURDAY 7TH DECEMBER - DIVISION TWO - HILLSBOROUGH (35,067)

SHEFFIELD WEDNESDAY 4-4 MANCHESTER UNITED

Stepney, Forsyth, Houston[1], Greenhoff, Holton (Davies), Buchan, Morgan, McIlroy, Pearson[1], Macari[2], McCalliog

Despite being third from bottom (and only one point above bottom club Millwall), Wednesday supporters turned up in their droves, more than doubling their previous best attendance of 15,295 and their heroes responded with a performance of

Sheffield Wednesday match magazine·price 10p

their own, though it was the league leaders who took the lead early on.

Stewart Houston was one of a pack of United players standing over a free kick and made it count, drilling it under the wall and into the net with just seven minutes gone. The Reds were in complete control for the few minutes that followed until Jim Holton was involved in a challenge with McCordie – Holton came off much worse, having to be replaced by Davies, and was later revealed to have suffered a broken leg. With concentration split between their performance and their injured colleague, United collapsed to three goals – David Sunley first from a corner, Colin Harvey with a splendid twenty-five yard volley from a free kick hoisted into the box that wasn't cleared, and then Bernard Shaw scored direct from a free kick awarded for a Lou Macari handball that appeared to be just inside the area. Harvey's goal had provoked delirium among Owls' fans and anger among United's away contingent, leading to fights between the supporters that temporarily spilled on to the pitch between the second and third Wednesday goals. The game continued until half time brought a natural break in play, although following Shaw's free kick, the United fans did stage a short pitch invasion, prompting the television commentator to suggest they were attempting to get the match abandoned.

It was the ideal time and opportunity for Docherty to have one or two words with his players and also reshuffle, moving Greenhoff to the back alongside Buchan. This has sometimes erroneously been referred to as a start of their legendary defensive partnership. Although technically Greenhoff and Buchan were playing alongside each other, it was a temporary fix for which Arnie Sidebottom was always the planned solution (as comically put after the game, Docherty quipped, "Of course it's a blow… it now means we're left with the second best centre half in the League, Arnie Sidebottom"). The Greenhoff/Buchan axis would have its secure development the following season although the impetus the team gained from having such an attack-minded player as Greenhoff in their back line at Hillsborough may well have planted the seed in the Doc's mind. United's response was instantaneous. McCalliog floated in a free kick from the left and it was headed back across goal by Davies; Wednesday keeper Peter Springett completely misjudged the situation and Lou Macari was left with a simple tap in.

Just before the hour mark, United were level – Morgan set Forsyth free on the right hand side, and the full back's cross was met with deadly accuracy by Pearson. It seemed for all the world that there would only be one winner with the Reds in the ascendancy but Wednesday were always a danger from set pieces – and, with twenty minutes remaining, they regained the lead through another, when Sunley headed in his second from a free kick that was swung in to the near post. United's relentless pursuit of another equaliser brought reward with nine minutes left. A free kick was hoisted into the box and met by Macari; his first effort was blocked by a home defender to the screams of 'handball' by hopeful away fans, but the diminutive Scot was composed enough to keep his balance and concentration in a busy penalty area to drive the ball past Springett and earn United a point in a 4-4 game that would go on to be remembered as one of the fondest memories of their time in the Division. Sports journalist Don Smith described it as "One of the most remarkable matches ever played at Hillsborough," while others concentrated on the violence, claiming that in excess of fifty arrests were made by half time. "One of the stewards went up to Tommy Cavanagh at full time and said to him, 'Get back over the hills and take your hooligans with you'," recalls Tommy Docherty. "Cav replied to him, 'We will, and next week, you'll be back to 15,000'."

"I'm not sure about it being the fondest memory, but certainly one of the most memorable was that away game at Hillsborough against Sheffield Wednesday. Now that had everything. Eight goals, a broken leg for big Jim Holton and a full scale riot in and around the stadium," remembers United fan Gary Thompson. "I remember getting off the football special at the little station at the top of the hill from the ground. There weren't many windows left intact by the time we got to the ground for sure."

Sadly for Holton the broken leg – in a season already disrupted by suspension and injury – was a significant setback from which his career would never fully recover. It was immediately clear that his season was over. "I don't expect Jim to play seriously again this season," said Docherty. "When I spoke to him after the game in hospital the first thing he wanted to know was the result in the match. That was before he even told me how he was feeling. Jim Holton also has character you see!"

The draw kept United five points clear at the top but had a far greater significance according to Docherty. He began his programme notes for the following game against Leyton Orient with the following bold statement, "Manchester United will be back in the First Division next season. I have never committed myself to that prediction so boldly before. On previous occasions I have said it is my ambition, my hope and my determination. But now I am sure we shall go back. I just know we will, and for the first time, I am saying so. The knowledge crystallised in my mind after our match at Sheffield Wednesday when the lads fought back from being 3-1 down to draw 4-4. The way they recovered from the blow of losing Jim Holton after the first quarter of an hour and then the three goals that were knocked past them inside 10 minutes, was truly inspiring. I have talked about the value of character in a team in these programme notes before and that was the quality shown by our lads at Hillsborough last week.

"No other club in the English League would have come back the way we did in those circumstances. It needed character. Our team has it and that is why I feel so confident now that we shall maintain the progress of the first half of the season and win our way back into the First Division… I think it is fair to claim that United motivate people. The Wednesday belied their position near the foot of the table and of course we had a 35,000 gate. I just wonder how many there will be at Hillsborough for their next home game. No doubt the attendance will drop considerably which must be very disheartening for their players. It will be very difficult for them to lift their game again. Fortunately Old Trafford does not have that problem. Our support allied with the character in the team will see us win promotion." Docherty's mood would be considerably worsened by what he described as 'parasite football' from United's next visitors.

SATURDAY 14TH DECEMBER - DIVISION TWO - OLD TRAFFORD (41,200)

MANCHESTER UNITED 0-0 LEYTON ORIENT

Stepney, Forsyth, Houston, Greenhoff (Davies), Sidebottom, Buchan, Morgan, McIlroy, Pearson, Macari, Daly

Try as they might, United were unable to break down the defensive wall of their visitors, restricted to speculative attempts that Orient 'keeper John Jackson was comfortable with. Docherty attempted to put extra pressure by bringing on Davies for Greenhoff but it was to no avail.

In fact, it might well have been worse for United. Late on, an Orient corner was headed in by Tom Walley, but it was ruled out for a reasons unclear to anyone but referee Roger Kirkpatrick. Kirkpatrick was then lovingly serenaded with chants of 'Kojak, Kojak' due to a generous perception that he resembled Terry Savalas – in fact, the name would follow him whenever he officiated at Old Trafford again. It was the most entertainment the home supporters enjoyed all afternoon.

Sammy McIlroy later reflected on the frustration of dropping a point. "Like against Portsmouth, it wasn't as if we had patience," says the Northern Irishman. "We were so disappointed, not just because we were expected to turn them over, but because we were on such a roll and we hadn't scored at Old Trafford. Orient were resilient and we might have been a little fortunate. To finish at 0-0 with a crowd roaring us on was so disappointing."

"They used pathetic tactics which, frankly, I wouldn't pay to watch," Docherty raged about his opponents, unable to find any amusement in the situation. "They are so pleased with themselves, you would think they had won the FA Cup."

Giving all due credit to the visitors who went away with what would be a famous result of their own, Docherty might later have observed that he had deployed all of his most goalscoring and inventive resources and that it just wasn't United's most penetrative day.

One might have put that down to a subdued performance from Willie Morgan, who used his 'Talkback' column in the club's newsletter to address being dropped earlier in the campaign. "Dear Willie," wrote Miss Jackie Withington from Stockport, "Quite a bit of publicity was given when you were recently substituted and then dropped from the side. How did this affect you and were you, as one paper implied, on the verge of a transfer request?"

With the kind of blunt honesty that is sorely lacking in the modern game, Morgan replied, "I'm very pleased you've asked this question Jackie. It gives me the opportunity to put the record straight. Certainly, being dropped from the team was a bitter disappointment – as it would be to any professional footballer. It hadn't affected me I might just as well have packed up playing. United had made a tremendous start to the season and I felt that I had played my part in the club's success. It was said that I was below form as a result of being involved in the World Cup finals during the summer and my eye injury prior to the start of the season. Personally, I disagreed with this view, but on reflection being dropped did me no harm in so much as I got a rest from the game. The last four years or so have been quite hectic for me both at club and international level."

With Middlesbrough being the next visitors to Old Trafford, one might feel it was a reasonable assumption that Docherty would welcome the higher calibre of opponent, with the mindset that Jack Charlton would be more confident of achieving a result. Not so, as the Doc now began to reason that the Reds' attacking force was feared by all in the game once more. "I know it is going to be a difficult match for us. When the draw was first made I rather fancied us to win at Ayresome Park because I felt that Middlesbrough would be more inclined to come out on the attack on their own ground," he wrote in his programme introduction. "This evening could see a different pattern of play and we shall have to be very careful that our visitors do not catch us on the hop and repeat the 1-0 win they scored here last season in the F.A. Cup. Jack Charlton has got his team extremely well organised and away from home they play with extra caution. So despite playing at Old Trafford, the replay could present a tougher proposition than the first game."

Charlton had more on his mind than how to set up his team. He had made a formal complaint to the FA regarding the appointment of Peter Reeves as referee – he had complained about his decisions in the first game, and felt he shouldn't take charge of the replay. Docherty felt the FA acted appropriately. "The Football League turned down his objection and in my opinion rightly so," opined Docherty. "I thought Peter Reeves was fair to both sides and had a good game at Ayresome Park. I know why Jack wanted a change of official and to a certain extent I sympathise. You see, Jack and I were brought up in a different football world. In our day there was an awful lot more physical challenge in the game. Tackling was an art and there was a fair amount of punishment handed out on both sides. In fact teams are fairies these days compared with most of the sides I played with and against. I imagine Jack Charlton, at least in his early playing days, would agree. Jack thought that the referee in our first game blew up for too many fouls which Jack would say were petty. But that is the way the game has changed and managers and players must accept it."

WEDNESDAY 18TH DECEMBER - LEAGUE CUP QUARTER-FINAL REPLAY
OLD TRAFFORD (49,501)

MANCHESTER UNITED 3-0 MIDDLESBROUGH

Stepney, Young, Houston, Greenhoff, Holton, Buchan, Morgan, McIlroy[1], Pearson[1], Macari[1], Daly
Sub : McCalliog

With 'Boro at full strength after being able to select three players who were unavailable for the first game due to suspension, and United under strength with Holton out and Forsyth replaced by Tony Young, the visitors should have been fully hopeful of repeating their Cup success of '73/74 and earning a semi-final place against Norwich City.

For most of the first half it seemed as if Docherty would be seeing his side held for a fourth successive game (humorously characterised in the 'FANatic' cartoon strip inside the match programme with the protagonist of the sketch shouting "TCH! ANOTHER ROTTEN DRAW!"). There could be no overwhelming argument to say United were battering Charlton's men but they earned the luck that brought the breakthrough through sheer persistence. Macari sent a free kick goalwards that looked harmless until 'Boro keeper Jim Platt made a boob, letting the ball slip through his hands and gifting an opportunity to Stuart Pearson. United's number 9 took it gleefully. If there had been reservations about Pearson since he signed from Hull, these were solely down to concerns over his fitness – his phenomenal goal return prompted the highest of compliments by one reporter who said the opener here was struck with 'Denis Law-like opportunism'.

With the game – and indeed tie – forced to open up for the first time, United were able to benefit massively on the counter attack. Middlesbrough were arguably bigger contributors to their own downfall, however, as it was another mistake that gave the Reds a stranglehold on the game. Souness slipped in possession and McIlroy was on it instantly, beating a man and sending the shot with aplomb into the Stretford End goal. United's best player on the night, Macari, got the goal he so richly deserved with a thumping volley to make it 3-0. "Super Reds on the glory road again," wrote *Daily Mirror* reporter Frank McGhee. "Only Norwich block their path to the League Cup final, which on last night's replay form makes me feel slightly sorry for Norwich," he continued.

United had halted the string of draws and managed to generate the momentum of that unbeaten run into a positive – Docherty was hoping that they could keep that up and achieve their first away win in four games at York City.

SATURDAY 21ST DECEMBER - DIVISION TWO - BOOTHAM CRESCENT (15,314)

YORK CITY 0-1 MANCHESTER UNITED

Stepney, Young, Houston, Greenhoff, Sidebottom (Davies), Buchan, Morgan, McIlroy, Pearson[1], Macari, Daly

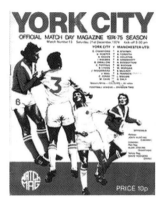

"Wishing You a Merry Christmas & a Happy New Year from us all at YORK CITY AFC, the friendly club," trumpeted the matchday programme. The festive spirit was continued inside by manager Tom Johnston who said, "So much has been written about this great

club that there is very little left to write, although at the present time the minority of trouble makers are getting more publicity than they deserve. I would rather applaud the majority of their supporters who have followed them in large numbers even if they have dropped a Division in the League. Most other Clubs would have had a big decline in gates." A generous profile on Tommy Docherty opened with "The graph on Tommy Docherty's remarkable career chart is sweeping rapidly upwards again as his United side leads the Second Division at a canter and looks certain to regain its place in the top section."

The generosity ended there. The six thousand travelling supporters were kept behind a fence behind one of the goals. "The club has spent £500 on the eight-foot scaffolding and wire mesh structure to enclose the end where most of United's supporters are expected to congregate. York are also worried that fear of the United fans' reputation – hardly enhanced by scenes at Hillsborough – will keep their own supporters away," wrote one report, claiming that 'hundreds of tickets' were still unsold.

Bootham Crescent's biggest gate of the season witnessed what was described by reporter Norman Wynne as a 'pathetic, guileless display' from York. "This was a friendly invasion with the Red army of fans on their best behaviour as they chanted United on their relentless march back to the First Division," wrote Wynne.

It had threatened to be another frustrating away trip for the Reds when Arnie Sidebottom was forced to come off early on, forcing Docherty into a tactical re-shuffle, putting Greenhoff back into defence. Ten minutes after the change, in the 18th minute, United had taken the advantage – Morgan the creator, and Pearson the finisher. It was the former Hull man's 10th goal in just 12 games, proving that when fit, he was worth every penny of the transfer fee Docherty had felt so justified in paying. That was all she wrote for this game – York never putting up a real fight to equalise, and United more than content to preserve their own energy and sit on the result.

Prior to the game, police escorted United supporters into their designated area – although some did find their way into other pockets of the ground, resulting in minor trouble – giving them a 'belt up' order. "The belt up warning is aimed at the foul mouthed fans whose obscene chanting is upsetting the real fans and club," wrote reporter Mark Humphreys. "United will embark on a New Year campaign, launched by the fans and backed by manager Tommy Docherty, to end the foul language. The idea of the Manchester United Supporters Club is to print song sheets compiled by fans as part of a competition. It is hoped the songs will replace the obscene chants. The plan will go into operation for United's first home match of February – against Bristol City – when around 20,000 song sheets will be distributed."

The song sheet was given its introduction in the fourth Supporters' Club newsletter of the season, with a lead in from Tommy Docherty. Supporters of a younger generation may already find the kind of comments spoken and printed by the football managers – and players, for that matter – in 1974 to be refreshing, honest and eye opening in stark contrast to the PR driven robotics of the modern age. However, one might think that's for the best when reading Docherty's comments here, and the way that fans may have reacted if similar words had been said to them when there was discussion about the Singing Section in 2013 and 2014.

"This is yet another venture by the supporters club designed for the benefit of you, the supporters, who have given such phenomenal support to Manchester United over years and it is certainly one worthy of success," wrote the manager. "For some reason unknown to me, supporters songs and chants have, over the past few years, appeared to be lacking in originality and have become more of an embarrassment to football clubs rather than an incentive. I can recall quite vividly attending matches at Old Trafford in the 1960's and hearing new songs from the Stretford End on each occasion. Some of those were classics in their own right, and it saddens me to find that they have now been replaced by present-day offerings, which, in comparison, are nothing short of 'rubbish'.

Some of the songs submitted are of a very high standard and I feel sure that they will all be given a 'fair hearing' by the most loyal supporters in football."

In all, the newsletter published 26 entries, and below are just a few highlights…

Lyrics : Miss Vivienne Lamb, Carlisle, Cumbria

Tune : "We'd Like To Teach The World To Sing"

We like to watch the lads we love,
Every Saturday.
To see them score,
How we adore
To hear us shout once more.

They know we'll always follow them,
Wherever they may go,
To watch them win
And hear us sing
Red Devils ever more.

Lyrics : F. Nash, Barnstaple, N.Devon – Tune : "Glory, Glory"

Glory, Glory Man United
Your football keeps us all excited
We have the greatest football team in the land

And United will go marching on.
Glory, Glory Man United,
Glory, Glory Man United,
Glory, Glory Man United,
On to victory.

Lyrics : Anthony Wilde, Blackley, Manchester

Tune : "National Anthem"

God bless our gracious team,
The best that's ever been,
God bless our team.
Let them score goals for us,
We think they're glorious,
God bless our gracious team,
God bless our team.

God bless our gracious boys,
Morgan, Pearson, and McIlroy,
God bless our boys
Keep Stepney on his toes
Let him save all the goals
God bless our gracious boys,
God bless our boys.

God bless our gracious fans,
They're best in all the land
God bless our fans.
Keep us all loyal and true
Let us keep smiling through,
God bless our gracious fans,
God bless our fans.

…and so it continued. Other highlights include two separate

entries to the tune of 'Viva Espana', 'Dad's Army' and 'My Way'. Sadly, none of the above managed to infiltrate themselves into the terrace jukebox.

Five points clear at Christmas, Reds were in plenty of cheer for the visit of West Brom on Boxing Day.

THURSDAY 26TH DECEMBER - DIVISION TWO - OLD TRAFFORD (51,104)

MANCHESTER UNITED 2-1 WEST BROM

Stepney, Young, Houston, Greenhoff, Sidebottom, Buchan, Morgan, McIlroy[1], Pearson, Macari, Daly[1+]

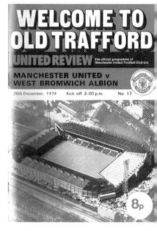

It was third time lucky for United – the first time in three attempts that the Reds had won a Boxing Day encounter at home. In front of the biggest crowd of the season, Sammy McIlroy gave his team an early lead in the fifth minute – drilling home from an angle, and catching out the keeper who was expecting a cross. McIlroy and Morgan were on top form, keeping the festive crowd warm by getting them to their feet on numerous occasions, but when the Baggies won a free kick just before the interval, Len Cantello drilled it past Stepney with the help of a deflection from Tony Young.

United's response in the second half was good and they arguably should have had two penalties. Referee Les Hayes awarded one, which looked soft compared to the other two incidents, for what he deemed to be a foul on Stuart Pearson. With a 100% record from the spot so far this season, Gerry Daly was never likely to miss and didn't – his strike preserved United's unbeaten record and maintained a five-point gap at the top of the Division.

Sadly, Docherty had been forced to confront the controversy of hooliganism once more in his match notes. "The game is going through a difficult period with a few people making life very difficult for the rest of us. The name of Manchester United has been bandied about in newspaper headlines lately in the kind of terms I hoped never to see associated with the club," he wrote. "And all because of the lunatic fringe of hooligans who have battened on to us. We have now reached the pitch where the Government feel it necessary to step in with directions on how to combat the problem."

The Christmas spirit seemed to escape local opponents, too. Elsewhere in the programme, Joe Lancaster reported on the Reserves 5-0 loss to Everton on December 14th. All the goals came in the second half, with Lancaster describing the game as 'all out war'. "Team boss Paddy Crerand, to save the Liverpool Constabulary the embarrassment of making an arrest on some of the Everton players for assault and battery, took McCreery off at half time," was his amusing recollection.

Sitting pretty at the top with a healthy lead of five points, United were in prime position to take advantage of the confidence that should have come with it. No doubt, Docherty and the team were hopeful that a good result in their last game of 1974 would give them the perfect springboard to see in the New Year. As it turned out, it did set the tone for results in January, but not in the way anyone connected with United would have hoped for or expected.

Despite Ian St. John's laughable claims that United were only worthy of similar fanfare to the likes of Oldham Athletic, even the Latics themselves were hardly likely to have any reservations in rolling out the red carpet for their nearby opponents. While they had indeed once graced the First Division, Oldham's last year in the top flight was over fifty years prior to the 1974/75 season, having been relegated in 1923 – some fifteen years before St. John was even born. They had spent the majority of the last twenty years between the Fourth and Third Division and, as their match programme pointed out perfectly, promotion to the Second was not even on the agenda at the start of the calendar year.

"The magic of Manchester United is such that today's date has always promised to be the highlight of our season at Boundary Park and we hope that the match itself lives up to all expectations," read the introduction in *Boundary News,* continuing, "… there cannot have been many people around at the start of 1974 who believed we had much chance of promotion, let alone winning the Third Division championship. For at the start of the year, we were lying 8th in the Third Division… 10 points behind third placed York City and 16 points behind leaders Bristol Rovers."

The opposition profile declared that United are 'probably the best known team in British football' and 'virtual certainties to return to Division One at the first attempt'. Elsewhere, home reporter Charlie Hocky put together a recollection piece from Oldham's record victory 12 Christmases' ago, when they beat Southport 11-0. "I'm looking for a repeat performance against United!" wrote Hocky, presumably with tongue firmly placed in cheek. That's not to say that hope of a home win was in the realms of fantasy – as indeed it turned out to be the case – but merely serves as confirmation that if there was, in fact, any delusion from anyone in football that Oldham deserved to be revered as much as the Reds for their accomplishments in football, it certainly wasn't the view held by anyone at Boundary Park.

SATURDAY 28TH DECEMBER - DIVISION TWO - BOUNDARY PARK (26,356)

OLDHAM ATHLETIC 1-0 MANCHESTER UNITED

Stepney, Young, Albiston, Greenhoff (Davies), Sidebottom, Buchan, Morgan, McIlroy, Pearson, Macari, Daly

As if to firmly underline the point, Oldham came into the game in 20th position in the league, just one point and two positions from the foot of the table. That said, the novelty factor of hosting United was probably wearing off, even for teams that had yet to come face to face with the Reds. Sheffield Wednesday – one place below Oldham – had recently got a point against United, as had Portsmouth, who were one place above them. Docherty's team were 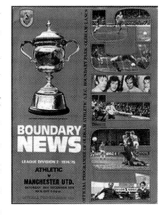 strong but not invincible, and with a young defence (Albiston at 17, Sidebottom at 20 and Young at 22), it was fairly evident that at times, they struggled with the uncompromising play of opponents who were always going to raise their game.

Considering the predicament that the hosts found themselves in, it would be wrong to suggest that their sole motivation was the honour of beating more illustrious opponents. To say that Oldham deserved their victory was an understatement. Not for the first time this season, a United game was decided by a penalty, though this time it was for the opposition. As the match entered the final quarter, Arnie Sidebottom handled in the area, and Maurice Whittle put the ball past Stepney. In fairness, United should have already been a goal down – with barely 10 minutes gone, Ronnie Blair's header beat Stepney, hit the stanchion and bounced out. To United's temporary relief, the referee didn't see it cross the line and waved play on. To this day, the 'ghost goal' is remembered fondly by Oldham supporters, though whether or not they would have the same sense of humour about it had it cost them what

Ronnie Blair's 'ghost goal' that was controversially disallowed.

eventually was a famous result is another matter altogether.

Docherty was left unimpressed. "So many of our ordinary League fixtures end up being played like Cup ties," he wrote in the following match programme. "Oldham are struggling in the League and yet they raised their game to win their first match for around 10 games against the leaders of the Second Division. And they did it with what I would call typical Cup football... hustling and chasing and getting stuck in to a degree that to my mind was bordering on the dangerous. Don't get me wrong. This is not sour

Maurice Whittle slams home the penalty to seal a famous Oldham victory

grapes because we lost. Oldham won because they got a penalty – which our player freely admits was right because he handled – while at the same time we didn't take our chances. I couldn't see the other controversial incident properly, but Alex Stepney says that the header that rebounded from our goal had also crossed the line and should have counted. So in that respect I am not cribbing about the result. It was a win for Oldham alright; what I am not so sure about is whether it was a win for football."

Much as he had cause to lament it given the fact it represented the biggest obstacle to his team's chances, in his more reflective moments Docherty would surely have conceded that those teams were simply using all of their resources to give themselves the best possible opportunity of achieving what, in many cases, would be a famous result, and having seen other clubs get favourable score lines adopting such tactics, no-one could blame teams for following suit.

Certainly, among the players, there was almost an expectancy that they would come up against these kind of performances. "It was just what we expected as players. In the First Division Manchester United were the biggest scalp so it was never going to be any different in the Second," confirms Macari. "It'd not been so long that United had Best, Law and Charlton so to get a result against those, no matter what age they were, there was tremendous kudos. Because a lot of those teams in the Second Division had not played against United, their efforts were even greater, as they were desperate to get a result against us."

The aggression which faced United was probably something that stood them in good stead for later years. First Division opponents were physical, some renowned for it in fact, but in the Second Division, United were finding that even though they were happy to get involved in a physical encounter, other teams would go that extra step further to compensate for the lack of quality that they had in comparison.

It was in defining where the line had been crossed which angered Docherty. "I have been perturbed on a number of occasions this season about the degree of physical play that is being allowed by some referees," he continued. "I am sure that there were a number of tackles in our match against Oldham that would have been booked by other officials. Ironically the one caution at Boundary Park was for kicking the ball away at a free kick. I don't condone that kind of behaviour, indeed players at Manchester United are fined for that kind of dissent. But it does seem out of perspective when other players are committing quite dangerous fouls. I am concerned about the way football is going. The authorities rightly clamped down on dangerous play such as the tackle from behind some time ago, but it is creeping back into soccer without being punished by every referee. It is this kind of inconsistency which so maddens managers. Referees must protect players in every match and this is not happening. Four or five times now teams have overstepped the mark against us and largely got away with it. There is little that we as a team can do about it. If we were to reply in kind there would be complete chaos with the game right out of hand and fans getting excited for the wrong reasons. Football would become total war and that is obviously not what we want. Football is entertainment and referees should bear this in mind. I am well aware that the accent in my team is on skill rather than robust play. It could be argued that I am trying to protect my players from football being a man's game. But I am not pleading for a namby pamby type of game. I was a very physical player myself, but times are changing and I honestly believe that the fans want to see creative, skilful soccer players allowed to flourish."

Docherty's comments suggested he felt a wider sense of responsibility - having been followed by the societal troubles that were associated with the game, it is perhaps no surprise that the manager was mindful of using the valuable space and time he did have to try and influence a change for the better. Even if he was still more than reasonably confident that he would take his club back into the First Division, there were still four months left in the Second to negotiate and so plenty of time for his concerns to bear fruit.

In ordinary circumstances, the prospect of facing Third Division opponents in the shape of Walsall at Old Trafford in the Third Round of the FA Cup might have seemed like a relief away from the hustle and bustle of League football, but taking into account Docherty's remarks, he was probably concerned that the aggression would be ramped up to its maximum in what was an actual, rather than allegorical, Cup tie.

The figurative honeymoon was most definitely over (and literal, too, for Stuart Pearson, who got married and went away for a quick trip between the Oldham and Walsall fixtures) as David Meek observed in his programme column. "… Even if they did drop a few points in December, every team has a slim spell. United's could well be behind them now," he suggested, on the eve of what would in fact turn out to be the Reds' most difficult period of the season.

IN RESERVE

IT WOULD TAKE a tremendous amount of exaggeration to seriously suggest that beyond the first team, Manchester United were blessed with world beaters throughout the reserves and academy in the mid 1970's. As is the case in the modern day at Old Trafford, standards are very different when it comes to United. Players are not only judged on their own potential but by their potential to emulate legends of the club. It is not an environment that should ever prove conducive to the development of young talent yet to say that it has always been normal at United is to request a certain flexibility of the term 'normal'; that is to say, for better or worse, players have to go through it, and it takes a certain type of character to succeed.

As we've already learned in travelling back through the first half of the 1974/75 season, Brian Greenhoff was earmarked as the next Bobby Charlton while David McCreery was being heralded as the best academy product since George Best (while two 'next George Bests', Sammy McIlroy and Willie Morgan, were still making their own names for themselves). From almost three hundred appearances, Greenhoff is most remembered for being one half of a fine defensive partnership. Like him, David McCreery made over one hundred appearances for United in a number of positions.

A successful academy can be defined in a number of ways; how many players make the first team, how many go on to have a professional career, and so on. For United's first FA Youth Cup game of the season, McCreery was joined in the starting line up by Arthur Albiston – both having recently made their first team debuts. Paul Bielby, at number 11, had already been given an opportunity at the age of just 17 in United's relegation season.

Jimmy Nicholl, the number four for the Reds' FA Youth Cup opener at Port Vale, played almost two hundred and fifty times for the club. And at the time, Lindsay McKeown and Jimmy Kelly were youth internationals for Northern Ireland and Scotland respectively. There was every reason to believe that from United's starting eleven of Ryan, McKeown, Bradley, Nicholl, Albiston, Fitzpatrick, Sutcliffe, McCreery, Botham, Kelly and Bielby, the club could rationally assume four or five would turn out to be useful players in the long term for the club. Three were - if we are to consider that Nicholl with 248 appearances and Albiston with 485 are real success stories, and McCreery (57) a good solid professional who justified his place at the club while he was there, then that should constitute as a good return from that year.

Of the trio, Albiston is arguably the most acclaimed and the most likely to feature in suggestions for a 'greatest ever' United XI, even if he is most likely to miss out in favour of the more successful Patrice Evra or Denis Irwin. Observers of Albiston in his prime may put up a strong argument for his inclusion, in much the same way as they might for Buchan or Greenhoff. Sentiment plays a part, of course, but at the same time, these are players who would probably have graced - and, perhaps even improved - the trophy laden United teams of the new century. This, however, is an argument or debate for another publication, and not one concentrating on the contemporary achievements of said players in the 1974/75 season. In closing on this note, and recognising accomplishments, it should also be noted that although Paul Bielby only made a couple more first team appearances, in 2007 he was given an MBE for his fine work in football with youngsters while Dave Ryan had a long working relationship with the club as a coach and working with their community endeavours.

With the benefit of hindsight it is perhaps difficult to comprehend that a team packed with players who would go on to play for the first team (or already had) couldn't manage to go further than they did in the FA Youth Cup. It was sad for Frank Blunstone that despite his highly commendable work, he was unable to have a Youth Cup win to his name – United hadn't won it since 1964, and it would be 1992 before they did again.

Despite that, he will have felt much pride at the development and progress of players such as McCreery considering that his primary objective was preparing players for the first team. Under the watchful eye of Jimmy Murphy, Blunstone seemingly welcomed the opportunity and challenge to be as actively involved in running the club behind the scenes.

It was perhaps in keeping with the season (at the level beyond the first team, at least) that United's chances of success in the Youth Cup were ended by Everton. The Toffees finished fourth in Division One that season and lost fewer games than anyone in the top flight. They finished three points behind champions Derby but eighteen draws from 42 games handicapped their own chances severely. They had significant strength in depth and proved a nuisance to United at the lower levels, not only knocking them out of the Youth Cup, but coming out victorious in two bruising reserve encounters while also knocking twelve goals past the Reds in two 'B' team games – including an 8-1 win.

Below is the entire list of results and scorers for the club's various teams beyond first team level in the 1974/75 season.

FA YOUTH CUP RESULTS

3rd Dec - 2nd Round   *Port Vale (A)*   *0-0*
9th Dec - 2nd Round replay Port Vale (H)   *3-0 Fitzpatrick, own goal*
    Sutcliffe

6th Jan - 3rd Round   *Newcastle Utd (A)*   *0-0*
8th Jan - 3rd Round Replay Newcastle Utd (H)   *2-0 Albiston, Sutcliffe*
11th Feb - 4th Round   *Everton (H)*   *0-1*

RESERVE TEAM RESULTS

Aug 17th	*Everton (H)*	*0-2*	
Aug 24th	*Burnley (A)*	*1-3*	*Sutcliffe*
Aug 27th	*Huddersfield Town (A)*	*1-2*	*Anderson*
Aug 31st	*Nottingham Forest (H)*	*2-0*	*McCreery, Graham*
Sep 2nd	*Bury (A)*	*2-1*	*McCreery, Bielby*
Sep 14th	*Sheffield United (H)*	*4-0*	*James, McCreery, Graham, Botham*
Sep 18th	*Bury (H) W*	*4-0*	*Sutcliffe, Anderson, Nicholl, Botham*
Sep 21st	*WBA (A)*	*1-1*	*Anderson*
Sep 28th	*Stoke City (H)*	*0-1*	
Oct 5th	*Blackburn Rovers (H)*	*2-2*	*Kelly, Young*
Oct 12th	*Leeds United (A)*	*2-2*	*Graham, Anderson*
Oct 14th	*Manchester City (H)*	*2-2*	*Martin, OG*
Oct 19th	*Huddersfield (H)*	*0-2*	
Oct 26th	*Blackpool (A)*	*1-1*	*Graham*
Nov 2nd	*Aston Villa (A)*	*2-2*	*Graham, Sutcliffe*
Nov 9th	*Wolves (H)*	*1-3*	*Kelly*
Nov 16th	*Coventry (A)*	*3-1*	*Kelly pen., Martin, Fitzpatrick*
Nov 23rd	*Derby County (H)*	*0-0*	
Nov 30th	*Liverpool (A)*	*2-4*	*Martin, OG*
Dec 7th	*Sheffield Wed (H)*	*1-1*	*James*
Dec 10th	*Sheffield United (A)*	*0-1*	
Dec 14th	*Everton (A)*	*0-5*	
Dec 21st	*Bolton Wanderers (H)*	*2-0*	*Nicholl, Kelly*
Dec 28th	*Newcastle (H)*	*2-1*	*Kelly, Lowey*
Jan 11th	*Sheffield Wed (A)*	*0-1*	
Feb 1st	*Wolves (A)*	*1-2*	*Davies*
Feb 8th	*Aston Villa (H)*	*3-0*	*Botham 2, Baldwin*
Feb 22nd	*Coventry (H)*	*2-1*	*McCreery, Anderson*
Mar 1st	*Nottingham Forest (A)*	*0-3*	
Mar 5th	*Manchester City (A)*	*1-1*	*Baldwin*
Mar 8th	*Preston (H)*	*0-2*	
Mar 12th	*Stoke City (A)*	*1-1*	*Nicholl*
Mar 15th	*Bolton (A)*	*0-0*	
Mar 22nd	*WBA (H)*	*0-2*	
Mar 26th	*Newcastle (A)*	*2-2*	*Martin, Loughnane*
Apr 5th	*Leeds (H)*	*0-1*	

Apr 7th	Liverpool (H)	0-1	
Apr 12th	Blackburn (A)	2-1	McCreery, Clark
Apr 19th	Blackpool (A)	2-2	Martin 2

'A' TEAM RESULTS

Aug 17th	South Liverpool (A)	3-1	Kirkup, Kelly, Lowey
Aug 24th	Wigan Athletic Res (H)	4-1	Kelly, Grimshaw, Botham, Loughnane
Aug 31st	Stockport County (A)	0-1	
Sep 7th	South Liverpool (H)	2-2	Botham, Bielby
Sep 14th	Liverpool (H)	0-2	
Sep 21st	Crewe Alexandra (H)	4-0	Kirkup, Kelly, Lowey, Storey
Sep 28th	Rochdale Reserves (A)	1-1	Smith
Oct 5th	Liverpool (A)	1-0	Loughnane
Oct 12th	Manchester City (H)	1-0	Morris pen.
Oct 19th	Southport Reserves (A)	2-3	Bradley, Bielby
Oct 26th	Manchester City (A)	2-0	Botham, Lowey
Nov 9th	Tranmere (A)	3-3	Storey, Bielby, Coyne
Nov 16th	Southport (H)	3-0	Storey, Bradley pen., Sutcliffe
Nov 23rd	Macclesfield (A)	0-3	
Nov 30th	Blackpool (A)	0-2	
Dec 7th	Morecambe (H)	5-0	Botham 2, Fitzpatrick, Bielby, Kirkup
Dec 21st	Stockport (H)	1-2	OG
Jan 4th	Preston (A)	4-0	Kelly, Lowey 3
Jan 11th	Preston (H)	9-0	Kirkup, Botham 3, Storey 2, Loughnane, Coyne, Clark
Jan 18th	Everton (A)	0-0	
Feb 1st	Tranmere (H)	1-1	Botham
Feb 8th	Wigan (A)	2-1	Coyne, Kelly pen.
Feb 15th	Chester (H)	1-0	Lowey
Feb 22nd	Chester (A)	3-3	Lowey 2, McKeown
Mar 1st	Rochdale (H)	1-2	Kirkup
Mar 8th	Crewe (A)	2-1	Lowey, Kirkup
Mar 15th	Morecambe (A)	2-2	Kelly, Botham
Mar 22nd	Macclesfield (H)	3-1	Lowey, Jackson, Fitzpatrick
Mar 29th	Everton (H)	0-0	
Apr 12th	Blackpool (H)	2-0	Kirkup, Jackson

B TEAM RESULTS

Aug 17th	Everton (H)	0-4	
Aug 23rd	Oldham Athletic (A)	2-2	Coyne, Loughnane
Aug 31st	Bolton Wanderers (H)	1-4	Beswick
Sep 14th	Burnley (A)	3-4	Bradley pen., Smith, Coyne
Sep 21st	Blackburn Rovers (A)	0-1	
Oct 5th	Manchester City (H)	0-2	
Oct 12th	Manchester City (A)	1-3	Jackson
Oct 19th	Wigan '(A)' (H)	3-1	Bailey, Loughnane, Smith
Oct 26th	Manchester City (H)	1-1	Kerr
Nov 2nd	Rochdale (H)	3-0	Botham, Storey, Grimshaw
Nov 9th	Tranmere (A)	0-2	
Nov 16th	Oldham (A)	0-1	
Nov 30th	Oldham (H)	0-5	
Dec 28th	Blackburn (H)	0-1	
Jan 11th	Crewe (A)	2-1	Phillips 2 pens
Jan 18th	Manchester City (A)	2-3	Coyne, Gilmour
Feb 1st	Liverpool (A)	2-6	Coyne, Thornley
Feb 22nd	Burnley (H)	1-0	Thornley
Mar 8th	Tranmere (H)	2-3	Coyne, Jackson
Mar 15th	Liverpool (H)	0-1	
Mar 18th	Rochdale (H)	2-1	Kelly, Kirkup
Mar 22nd	Bolton (A)	1-0	Phillips pen.
Mar 29th	Everton (A)	1-8	Jackson
Apr 5th	Crewe (H)	4-0	Loughnane 2, Coyne, Jackson
Apr 12th	Bolton (A)	2-1	Griffiths, Novacki
Apr 19th	Oldham (H)	4-2	Clarke 3, Coyne

LANCASHIRE YOUTH CUP

Sep 30th	First Round	Blackburn R (H)	1-0	Mccreery
Nov 12th	Second Round	Man City (A)	2-1	Botham, Kelly
Mar 3rd	S-Final 1st Leg	Preston (H)	0-0	
Mar 11th	S-Final 2nd Leg	Preston (A)	3-1	Mccreery, Kelly, Kirkup
Apr 16th	Final 1st Leg	Everton (H)	2-1	Kelly Pen., Storey
Apr 23rd	Final 2nd Leg	Everton (A)	1-0	Storey

MASTERMIND

THE CLUB'S OFFICIAL newsletters were full of helpful and interesting information – there was an in-house Quiz Team captained by John Gray, and John set some questions that were under the Categories of Difficult and Easy in 'U–NI–TED' Volume 6 Number 1.

In Volume 6, Number 2, Alex Stepney assumed the position of "Quiz master" for the First Round of the 'Mastermind Football Quiz'. "The competition is open to all supporters club members and the only stipulation is that no reference books should be used when answering the questions. Members who are tempted to look the answers up should note that as the competition progresses questions will be asked over the phone and the Final rounds will in fact be 'live'" the newsletter stated.

MASTERMIND - FIRST ROUND

As a rough guideline for answering the Mastermind questions, members should allow themselves approximately 30 seconds for each question. This is the normal time allowance which the club quiz team has experienced in past competitions.

1. *In which year were International Caps first introduced?*
2. *Name the first team to win all 21 'home' League games in a season?*
3. *Who were the first winners of the Football League Cup?*
4. *Which team won the World Club Championship in 1970?*
5. *Which two teams played in the 1952/53 Amateur Cup Final?*
6. *Which two teams played in the first European Champions Cup Final, and where was the game played?*
7. *Name the goalscorers in the 1962 World Cup Final?*
8. *Name the current United player who holds the record for scoring in League football.*
9. *Name the England team which lost to the U.S.A. in 1950?*
10. *Who won the Scottish First Division in 1964/65?*

MASTERMIND - SECOND ROUND (from Volume 6, Number 3)

1. *What is the record score in a full International match in Britain. Name the two countries and the year?*

2. *Which player commanded the first £1,000 transfer fee?*

3. *Which country beat England for the first time on foreign soil and in which year?*

4. *Name the first goalkeeper ever to captain England?*

5. *Who held the record for International caps for England before being passed by Billy Wright?*

6. *Which was the first English League game to be played under floodlights?*

7. *Name England's first ever substitute?*

8. *Who scored six goals for The Football League against The Irish League, at Wolverhampton in 1952?*

9. *Which team did Cambridge United replace when they were elected to the Fourth Division?*

10. *Name the first 'closed-circuit' televised game in this country. And which year?*

A few 'two-part' questions included this month. A half-mark will be given for each part of the question answered, so don't worry if that's all you can answer.

MASTERMIND - THIRD ROUND (from Volume 6, Number 4)

1. *In which year were professional players first recognised?*

2. *Which League club had 3 players 'sent-off' in one match last season?*

3. *What was the highest score in the First Division last season?*

4. *What was special about the Cambridge v. Oldham match in season 1973/74?*

5. *In which year did Liverpool reach the Final of the European Cup Winners' Cup?*

6. *For which team did Terry Bly play when he scored 52 goals in 1960/61?*

7. *Name the winners of the first F.A. Challenge Trophy?*

8. *Who scored the first goal in the first F.A. Cup Final played at Wembley?*

9. *How many penalties have been awarded in F.A. Cup Finals at Wembley?*

10. *In which season did the numbering of players become compulsory in the Football League?*

Welcome to the final MASTERMIND of this season. All members should note that this is the last opportunity for you to enter for the MASTERMIND FINAL, to be played early next season.

MASTERMIND - FOURTH ROUND (from Volume 6, Number 5)

1. *Name the two teams who played in the 1960/61 European Cup Winners Cup Final?*
2. *Name the scorers in the above match?*
3. *How many caps did Duncan Edwards gain for England?*
4. *Name the winners of the 1971 FA Youth Cup Final?*
5. *In which year did Wilf Smith sign for Coventry City?*
6. *Who scored Liverpool's goals in the 1970 FA Cup semi-final at Old Trafford?*
7. *In what year was the roof covering all 100,000 spectators at Wembley completed?*
8. *Name the first ever FA Cup Final substitute?*
9. *In which year did United play City in the Charity Shield?*
10. *Name the venue for the 1966 European Champions Cup?*

TALKBACK

Another popular feature of the Newsletters was "Talkback" where supporters were invited to send in questions to a selected player. Here are some of the highlights.

ALEX STEPNEY (Volume 6, Number 2, November 1974)

John Hopkins, Aylesbury, Bucks., writes;
Last season and again this season it is noticeable that more emphasis is placed on throwing the ball rather than kicking it. I imagine this is in order to keep possession, but have you found it necessary to practice throwing the ball or has it come naturally?

"Well John, it's quite true that more emphasis has been placed on throwing the ball rather than kicking it in order to keep possession, but this is nothing new to me. I always used to throw the ball out, particularly when

Pat Crerand was in the side. When Paddy finished playing I found that other players preferred me to clear the ball by kicking it and until recently I used to do this. Now, of course, there's been a return to the throw and this stems from Tommy Docherty, who wants us to be involved in each game as much as possible and the more we keep possession the less chance of the opposition breaking through to score. I wouldn't say that I've had to practice throwing accurately. This is a basic necessity for every goalkeeper."

Charles Farringia writes from Zurrieg, Malta;
When United return to the First Division next season how do you think they will go on?

"I definitely like your confidence Charles. Rather than sound too optimistic though can I just say that the present United side would do very well indeed in today's First Division. The confidence and ability of the players in the team, in particular the youngsters, has really shone through this season and I would confidently expect United to finish in the top half of the table."

WILLIE MORGAN (Volume 6, Number 3, December 1974)

James Bodin, Newbury, Berkshire would like to know;
"Why is it that you rarely overlap down the wing when United are attacking. By holding back I always feel that the opportunity to stretch the opposing defence is wasted."

"I fully appreciate your point of view concerning this James, but it is one of the many tactics of modern-day football which is not fully appreciated by supporters. All modern-day defences are very difficult to split, regardless of which division you're playing in and very little room is available down either flank. This is why there are so few orthodox wingers in the game. Mind you, I do go wide when the opportunity arises and I'm always

prepared to go down the line and beat the full-back when there is sufficient space and freedom."

Christine Moss, Reading, Berks, asks;
"What's the most memorable goal you've ever scored?"

"That's a fairly easy one to answer Chris. I'm not what you could describe as a prolific goalscorer so there's not too many to choose from. I recall the goal I scored against Birmingham in the FA Cup fifth round at Old Trafford in the 1968/69 season as probably my best ever. We won the game 6-2 and I scored the sixth at the Stretford End beating a few players on the way to goal (a somewhat modest description - Ed). I remember it was the start of a busy week for us at the time. We played Rapid Vienna in the European Cup on the Wednesday and in the next round of the FA Cup against Everton at Old Trafford on the Saturday we were beaten 1-0 - the ball 'hitting' Joe Royle's leg for the only goal."

LOU MACARI (Volume 6, Number 4, February 1975)

Next question from Miss Gillian Beck, Hindringham, Norfolk.
"Although you are not very tall, you seem to tower above defenders in the penalty area. How do you manage to keep outjumping your opponents?"

"There's only really one answer to that Gillian. Being confronted by massed defences, especially in the penalty area, the days of making space for oneself have virtually gone, and it's all a question of timing. Knowing when to make the move is one of the most important training facets of any of today's strikers."

Colin Loader, Welwyn Garden City, Herts.
"Dear Lou, You are scoring more goals this season. Do you think the presence of Stuart Pearson has helped you?"

"Well Colin, obviously the more players up front when we are attacking, the better the chances we have of scoring goals. Stuart certainly helps take the pressure off myself and the other forwards, which allows us that extra freedom in which to create and take any chances that come our way. "

MARTIN BUCHAN (Volume 6, Number 5, May 1975)

Ann Ravenscroft, Lower Broughton, Salford writes;
"I've noticed that when you lead the team onto the pitch before a match you are the only one not wearing a track-suit top. Is there any special reason for this?"

"Dear Ann, All the other players wear a certain make of boots and wear track-suits made by the manufacturers. I prefer a different brand of footwear and so do not advertise the boots that the rest of the lads use."

Next question from Miss Doreen Preston, Kings Heath, Birmingham;
"Personally speaking, I haven't yet seen a player who can out-run you for the ball. Do you do extra training for this?"

"Dear Doreen,
It's funny you should think I'm very fast, because I think that at least half the lads in the team can beat me at running. Maybe because I play at the back and have more time to see things happen and position myself I look a lot quicker than I really am. I certainly don't do any special training, just the same as the rest of the team."

JANUARY

HEADING INTO CHRISTMAS, United manager Tommy Docherty had given the real first public indication of his belief that his team would be heading straight back into the First Division, in spite of what he perceived to be an over-zealous approach to stopping his side playing from opponents. Jumping back in time to his first programme notes of the season, it is clear to see that even if he was dissatisfied with the game plan of rival clubs, he was well prepared for it to happen.

"Man for man I think we can compare with every other team in the Second Division, but of course this is not the whole story," he explained. "We must capture the right attitude and match the spirit and working rate of our opponents. This is a hard division, certainly harder to get out of than to fall into. I have worked in the Second Division and know the problems. You have got to decide which teams you can play football against and those which require you to make increased physical effort. Against some sides it is necessary to run, chase and work, and let the football flow if you can find the time. It has always been fashionable to try and beat Manchester United. This will be especially so in the Second Division when we meet old friends who have fallen on old times and when we play against new faces anxious to impress against a club with probably the most famous name in the game."

He could not have been more accurate and it was a perfect verse for United's players to adopt as their mantra. But footballers are human, and cannot help but be swayed by momentum and events in games as they come either individually or in a row.

At the beginning of the 1974/75 season United began like a house on fire, plundering goals against wide-eyed opposition at Old Trafford and catching home sides unawares with their counter attacking philosophy. It seemed, for a while, as if only spoiling or complacency would undermine chances of instant promotion. Any team heading down into the Second Division after a long stay in the top flight are seen as scalps. But Manchester United aren't 'any team' and for many clubs they were coming up against, they weren't just the biggest game of the season, but arguably a generation. It's easy to understand why players could be motivated and also overwhelmed contemporaneously.

As the Doc observed, it's always been fashionable – for any team, regardless of stature – to beat Manchester United. With all due respect, there was always the high probability that United's quality would prove too much for most of the teams in the Second Division. No team can have a perfect season, and none ever have in English professional football. Preston North End's 1888/1889 'Invincible' League campaign was followed by Arsenal's unbeaten season of 2003/2004 but neither side won every single game (though, through virtue of winning the FA Cup the same season, and thus not losing a single game in any competition, Preston's is arguably still the closest to perfect that any have come). United, though, have always carried the expectation of having to win every single game.

As they embarked upon their journey in the lower league, Docherty had uncertainty in himself, and maybe even in his team. After all, he was openly aware of the difficulties which faced his team. And with that in mind, United showed fighting spirit in their opening games which perhaps caught their opponents off guard. As their quality – and the difference in quality – became more evident, it is only reasonable that United's players became more confident. As did Docherty. And over time, with their style of play captivating their supporters in the traditional fashion that they had become accustomed to, and the old arrogance returning to their charismatic off-pitch leader, it is natural to assume that the fighting spirit dissipated.

That is not to say that United didn't fight hard on the pitch. Results proved otherwise. But there is enough to suggest, in remarks like the ones made by Macari about how easy he found the division in retrospect, that at least subconsciously, the players' confidence had risen enough to feel that based simply on quality, they should win games in relative ease. They grew into life in the Second Division, but the same could not be said in return – while the novelty of having United in the league may well have been wearing off by the turn of the year, each club only got two opportunities to play them, meaning it was still a relatively new experience for them. By Christmas, with some clubs observing what it took to get a result from them, United were facing similar game plans almost every week.

Considering themselves now above the kind of dogfight which they had once expected, they had become indifferent to it, which in turn only served as further motivation to opposition players who felt they had discovered a way to get under the skin.

That is the more considered argument for United's struggles at this part of the season. It may be just as logical to suggest that the winter pitches – particularly in the Second Division – proved a distinctive leveller, and in some cases, actually may have provided an advantage to teams so used to playing at that level in their own style over a number of years. It could not be reasonably argued that playing surfaces in Division One were anything like the immaculate bowling greens of the modern era but bad pitches and uncompromising opposition were two major ingredients of a perfect storm. United, forced into playing a young team and rarely a settled eleven, struggled through this new territory with a fledgling side.

There is, of course, another explanation.

A final look back to those initial programme notes for the

first home game against Millwall gives an intriguing insight to the level of change United had undergone. Docherty had counted 34 players that had left since he had taken charge fifteen months previously, not including George Graham. There had been suggestions of discontent behind the scenes earlier in the season, particularly with the Willie Morgan situation, and it was during the winter that the issues between Morgan and Docherty reached a peak. Prior to the 1974 World Cup, Docherty had reckoned that there was not a 'better player in his position in English football, nor the world' than Morgan.

On Saturday, 4th January, 1975, the relationship between the two reached their deepest low yet.

In the match programme for the FA Cup game with Walsall, club secretary Les Olive made a special announcement that all United's away games for the rest of the season would be all ticket, with no tickets available on the day of the game, in order for authorities to better segregate home and away supporters on the day of the game. "What we wish to make very clear is this," Olive wrote. "That it is up to our supporters to behave in a proper manner and conduct themselves as good representatives of our Club. This

The Scottish Old Trafford contingent in happier times

applies whether it is at the away ground, whilst travelling to and from the opposing city or whilst in the towns between the station and the ground. The onus is everyone as, if there is any outbreak of violence, then we will immediately be forced to restrict the sale of tickets to Season Ticket holders, League Match book holders and through the Supporters Organisations."

SATURDAY 4TH JANUARY - FA CUP THIRD ROUND - OLD TRAFFORD (43,353)

MANCHESTER UNITED 0-0 WALSALL

Stepney, Young, Houston, Greenhoff, Sidebottom, Buchan, Morgan, McIlroy, Pearson, Macari, Daly

Sub : Davies

"This afternoon it's the glamour and the excitement of the F.A. Cup," wrote Docherty. "There is nothing quite like it. We are delighted to have reached the semi-finals of the League Cup and we are thrilled by our progress in the promotion campaign. But I guess there will be an even extra sparkle today as we welcome Walsall to Old Trafford for a third round tie in the F.A. Cup. I have no doubt that the Midlands Third Division club all also be sniffing the Cup

air with extra appreciation and that we shall be in for a hard match. Whatever Walsall throw at us cannot possibly come as a surprise to us this season."

Maybe so – but it wouldn't have made it any less frustrating an afternoon. Walsall treated the game as if they too were a Second Division club but only in the respect that they were determined to get a home and away encounter with United. It was a strong side Docherty was able to field – the more experienced Houston recalled – but they found the intractable defence of their visitors impenetrable.

Of the many games United had found themselves chasing in recent weeks, this appeared to be one too far, and the lack of imagination in their attack prompted Docherty to shock the home crowd by hauling off Morgan for Davies. Similar gambles had already worked for the manager this season but not this time; the hosts were restricted to set pieces for their best openings, with a Houston effort the closest they came. Following Morgan's withdrawal, Walsall opened up slightly and actually had the better opportunities of the second half.

Reports after the game suggested that with the fixture pile up caused by United's League Cup run, a replay was the last thing that Docherty wanted – an ironic subtext to Walsall's late adventure which contradicted their initial intentions. United were in the hat for the fourth round draw and still favourites to proceed. Asked if he'd be looking for a lucky draw in the next round, Docherty quipped, "We had one today! We can't expect two in one day."

If on pitch events weren't exactly playing second fiddle to behind the scenes drama, the troubles Docherty now faced with Morgan (which were self inflicted by virtue of the manager's team selection) were probably ones he could have done without at this time in particular.

TUESDAY 7TH JANUARY - FA CUP THIRD ROUND REPLAY - FELLOWS PARK (18,105)

WALSALL 3-2 MANCHESTER UNITED (AET)

Stepney, Young, Houston, Greenhoff, Sidebottom, Buchan, McCalliog, McIlroy[1], Pearson, Macari, Daly[1+]

Sub : Davies

As United progressed in the League Cup, Docherty made a point to address speculation that the club could do without the distraction of Cup runs. The manager stressed that with the carrot of European football as the motivation, and United's eagerness to return to premier competitions as quickly as possible, there would be no complacency and certainly no purposeful defeat. One can't help but surmise that privately, if defeat was to occur, then Docherty would have wanted it to be done as quickly as possible

(though avoiding defeat at Old Trafford did at least preserve the unbeaten record there this season). In the event, it took as long as it possibly could.

Club Captain Doug Fraser, in the Walsall programme, wrote, "Possibly with a little more care in front of goal we could have won, but I'm delighted to bring back such a fine team to Fellows Park. Our loyal supporters deserve such an attraction. If the match is played in the same spirit and sporting way as at Old Trafford you won't be disappointed. Tonight could be a feast for you all." Fraser also claimed that Docherty had personally approached them after the first game. "Manager Tommy Docherty congratulated us after the match and said we were the only team to come to Old Trafford this season and deserved to go away with some reward." If true, Docherty probably reasoned that the invention of the visitors in the latter stages deserved at least a pat on the back – teams treating League games like Cup ties may have frustrated him, but it was by the very nature of the cliché expected in a knockout competition that teams would sometimes play for a replay. The suggestion of an entertaining game, however, may well have been made more in hope than expectation give the deadlock that transpired in the first game and the fact that neither team had scored in their previous league game before, either.

Thankfully – for Walsall and neutral supporters – it didn't take long for this game to flare into life. Bernie Wright, the former Everton player, positively smashed in a 21st minute strike from a cross by Brian Taylor. United were able to respond 10 minutes before half time after Stan Bennett was harshly determined to have handled the ball in the area. Gerry Daly had a perfect record from his eight penalties previously, and made no mistake with his ninth.

Level at half time, the fifteen minute break arguably saw greater drama than the following forty-five. Willie Morgan had been named in the original starting eleven but Docherty had changed his mind and gone with McCalliog instead. A story in 'The Doc's Devils' explains Morgan claimed that he tried to give some advice to Alex Forsyth at half time (though neither were playing) and Docherty apparently said, "You've got your own troubles without telling him how to play." If the chronological placing of this exchange of words appears insignificant, it becomes clearer in events that followed.

Conscious that his opponents may well be satisfied with another draw, thus bringing around a second replay and another payday, Docherty made a decision early in the second half to bring off goalscorer Daly and bring on Davies. "Walsall by then were looking for another replay. I wasn't, so I decided to do something different," said the manager. Unfortunately for him, he got the next worst thing to a replay, and that was an extra time period that brought further unwanted energy draining. An uneventful first period was followed by a quarter of an hour where the game, and tie for that matter, finally sprung into real life. Alex Stepney made an uncharacteristic howler, dropping a cross that fell at the feet of a delighted Alan Buckley. Buckley was never going to miss.

Six minutes later, Walsall were awarded a penalty when Martin Buchan brought down George Andrews - Buckley kept his cool to double his tally and his team's lead. United responded instantly and fortuitously got a way back into the game when an attempted clearance ricocheted off McIlroy into the goal. With five minutes to go, United now poured forward in search of the second replay which Docherty was so reluctant to see, but were unable to find an equaliser.

"Manchester United's F.A. Cup run was short and sweet!" wrote David Meek. "But it may be a good thing in the long run as the Reds turn into the last lap for promotion and face up to two testing legs in the semi-final of the League Cup." The following day, newspapers were full of columns suggesting that Docherty was in fact pleased about United's exit as it removed an unwanted distraction. If pleased might be something of an exaggeration, then there was at least that consolation of the semi-final in the League Cup on the horizon. He wouldn't have exactly been beaming that Wednesday as Morgan went to see him and said that he felt that it was pointless him continuing as captain.

It was back to the bread and butter for United and the return game against Sheffield Wednesday for their first home league game since Boxing Day (though, incidentally, Altrincham's Cup replay with Everton was held at Old Trafford on the same evening of the Walsall replay. A special edition of *United Review* was printed, a four page document profiling both teams and listing team-sheets on the back).

Docherty and Morgan's relationship continued to dominate the mood behind closed doors as Wednesday came to Old Trafford. "In front of all the other players in the dressing room, he (Docherty) apologised. That was quite a gesture and shows how unpredictable he is," remembers Morgan, who was recalled to the starting line up. The lord gave, and the lord hath taken away – the winger may have been recalled, but Docherty had taken him at his word and decided to name a new captain.

The identity pleased others in the team. "He was replaced by Martin Buchan. I thought it was the right decision, as Willie was being disruptive, his anger towards the Doc was plain to see and it wasn't pleasant," recalled Brian Greenhoff in his autobiography. "Martin was a natural leader and a steadying influence, he would fight the corner for the players and went on to become a fantastic captain. If there was ever any problem with the players he'd go to the management and sort it out. On the field, if we had to make decisions he would do it. Martin was a natural – the perfect captain for us." Greenhoff may well have been disappointed to not have been named captain - in Willie Morgan's absence of the pre-season tour of Belgium and Denmark, he had been named captain even with Buchan in the side. "I would have loved it, but I could never say Martin was the wrong choice," admitted the Barnsley-born star later. Lou Macari's status as a big money player may well have seen him as a contender. "I think it was more of a symbolic thing and it didn't really matter who got it when Willie lost it. It was almost irrelevant," he insists. "That said, the best man for the job was Martin Buchan because he was somebody you could rely on week in, week out. Martin wasn't everybody's cup of tea, some didn't find him easy to deal with, but I always found him okay. He was his own man, and there was no problem with that."

The appointment of Buchan was something of a masterstroke by Docherty. In the years that passed there became a clear divide in players who would either speak well, or speak ill, of their old manager. Some are happy for their dislike of him to be known; some are unapologetically fond of him. It could never be said that Buchan was a sycophant as he was very much his own person. This much is confirmed by the man himself. "Some other players were part of the Doc's inner circle but I certainly wasn't," said Buchan.

In conversation for this book he elaborated. "Maybe it was just about standing up for the right thing rather than being awkward or taking on a battle that you won't win," he says. "I'm sure he might have thought I was an awkward so and so but I just questioned things. If asked to jump, some players would just say, "How high boss?" I'd say "Why do you want me to jump?" and if he gave me a good reason, I'd jump higher than anybody else on the team. I just wouldn't do things blindly. As long as I believed in it, I'd do it to the best of my ability. I'm not a saint, but there were certain things I believed in and stood up for, and if Doc respected me for that, then I'm pleased."

Strong-willed and opinionated, and an obvious leader on the

pitch, it could stand to conventional logic that in another world Docherty could have identified Buchan as a trouble-maker. That is not to say that he ever was, or indeed ever threatened to be (even taking into account the pre-season passport incident), but strong individual characters do not always bond, and sometimes the nature of that strength can create divides when disagreements occur as they inevitably do in human relationships. In some ways, then, it was something of a bold choice for Docherty to name the best man for the job rather than reward one of his 'favourites' in the team (even if, in the case of Greenhoff, there was also a logical explanation as to why he could have been given the armband), but the bottom line is that Docherty was simply a good football manager who, by and large - and certainly at this time - made the right decisions at Manchester United.

Even this, though, has been challenged. "At training one morning (during the '74/75 season), Docherty was ranting and raving during the practice match and Buchan yelled, 'The way you're going, you're not helping things.' Docherty sent him off and they've had repeated verbal clashes in the dressing room," recalled Morgan. In 'The Doc's Devils', author Sean Egan suggests that in fact Buchan might and possibly should have been named skipper before, but that his 'stubborn and individualistic streak' might have delayed the appointment. An alternative theory might be that Docherty admired the righteousness in Buchan and, to an extent, might have seen something of himself in him. Those theories were all put to Buchan forty years later in the construction of this book and he gives a typically fascinating background and story. "I can't remember any meeting where I was told I would be captain, I must admit," he says. "But Willie had been captain for a while and then he was out of favour so Doc needed a new one... I had been used to that, too. For a while, I'd been played out of position, with Clive Griffiths, the Welsh lad in my place at number six. I just got on with it. I actually captained Manchester United in my first home game after joining them. I remember that clearly. On Wednesday 8th March 1972, against Everton in front of 38,000 in the afternoon. They couldn't use the spotlights because of the restrictions on the use of electricity with the power strikes. Bobby had been captain but was injured at Spurs on my debut the previous Saturday. I wasn't going to question it and I wasn't ever going to turn down the captaincy when it came as a permanent appointment. Even though Willie had been having his problems with Doc the thought of the captaincy coming up was not anything I ever thought about. But like I say, I wasn't going to say no."

Buchan was elated to be asked but also felt that he had earned the right. "I was very happy to be asked," he confesses. "I was captain at Aberdeen so it wasn't something I hadn't done before or something I wasn't comfortable with. My dad always said there should be 11 captains on the pitch. I always felt of it more an honour than an onus... some players don't have the personality or desire to be in that position. I'd had a very good education in the game. The Aberdeen manager. Eddie Turnbull, who taught me the game... he was the best coach that ever lived. I played in a good team there. We were the second best team in Scotland to a very good Celtic team, who'd been European finalists in 1967 and again in 1970. We beat them in the Scottish Cup Final in 1970 and also beat them at Parkhead 10 days before the final. I was captain on both occasions so it wasn't new. If you understand the game, you can try and change things if they're not going well, or get to a player to raise their game. You have to put it right as quick as you can because you can't afford to wait for half time for the manager or coach to intervene and it's too late at full time. Every manager I ever played for was quite happy to tell the players that if they saw that things weren't going right, to sort it out, and do it with confidence."

At 24, Buchan was the right age to lead a group of players that were by and large either the same age or just a little younger – before, perhaps he was just not experienced enough despite his role at Aberdeen to have been considered to succeed Bobby Charlton or George Graham before Willie Morgan got the role. Once the 'deadwood' had been cleared, Buchan was clearly a popular choice among his team-mates for the role because of the way he conducted himself though he insists that that was not a conscious act. "I was just being me. I wish I was organised as much now as I was back then! I wasn't quite OCD but I liked things doing right and my own way. I'd clean my own boots – well, I'd let the apprentices clean my training boots, but I'd clean my own match boots myself," he says.

Moving on to the selection for the following game – Docherty's alleged apology to Morgan before the fixture with Sheffield Wednesday could be perceived as an attempt to put everything right between the pair and create a more positive environment going into the only home league game of January.

SATURDAY 11TH JANUARY - DIVISION TWO - OLD TRAFFORD (45,662)

MANCHESTER UNITED 2-0 SHEFFIELD WEDNESDAY

Stepney, Forsyth, Houston, Greenhoff, James, Buchan, Morgan (Daly), McIlroy, Pearson, Macari, McCalliog[2+]

It could also be reasoned that Morgan was recalled for the same reason of resolution and moving on (particularly because he kept his place in the side from this point) but no definitive conclusions could be drawn from the selection for this game seeing as Docherty was forced to make a number of changes, reflecting the problems caused by the replay against Walsall.

The experienced Steve James was in the team ahead of Sidebottom, marking his first appearance of the season. Tony Young was dropped in favour of Forysth, while Morgan's return to the team meant that Gerry Daly had to settle for the substitute's role.

"Promotion is the priority at Old Trafford this season and while a Cup run is marvellous I don't want too many distractions from the main objective," wrote Docherty in his match-day column. "January is certainly a Cup month with our first semi-final in the League Cup at Old Trafford on Wednesday followed by the visit to Norwich for the second leg the following week. I just hope that we can keep our concentration on our League fixtures as well… starting again this afternoon with the visit of Sheffield Wednesday. It was at Hillsborough where we shared those epic eight goals last month and where Jim Holton broke his leg of course. Perhaps I could take this opportunity of repeating for our friends from Sheffield that Jim was the first to admit that his injury was a complete accident. That goes for us all at Old Trafford. It was just one of those unlucky, unfortunate things that happen in football every now and then… The Hillsborough match was quite remarkable with the way the scoring went. I don't think we can promise anything quite as high scoring this time, but I am sure we can look forward to a keenly fought game. Wednesday seem to be having a difficult time down near the bottom of the table and they were also set back with an F.A. Cup defeat at Chelsea last week. But don't let this kind of situation fool you! Regularly teams raise their game when they are playing the leaders of the Second Division… That is how it goes these days for Manchester United. Nothing that Sheffield Wednesday could produce today would surprise me!"

As thrilling as the first game between the sides was, sometimes, straightforward victories can be a welcome break from the excitement, and that was exactly what the 45,000 plus crowd (the highest in England on the day, again) were treated to, for want of a better phrase. In the 21st minute, Sammy McIlroy's fantastic overhead kick was stopped from going in by a handball on the line from Wednesday's Jimmy Mullen. Mullen was booked, and with Daly unavailable, it was left to Jim McCalliog to take up penalty duties. His effort sent the 17 year-old Owls keeper Peter Fox the wrong way. Reporter Bert Thorpe described Mullen's effort as 'the second best save of the day' and also revealed that both Mick Prendergast and Fred McIver in the Sheffield Wednesday team were wearing number ten! "The only effect it had was to inspire newly-elected skipper Martin Buchan to keep them both in check," wrote Thorpe.

Whether it was because there was little else to note in the game in terms of real excitement - bar McCalliog's stunning solo second just after the break where he sauntered through the visitors defence to drill past Fox, which sealed the 2-0 scoreline (the striker lamented his inability to get a third, saying "I was dying to get a hat-trick at Old Trafford") - or a sudden new found appreciation for Buchan's unsung ability because of the news of the captaincy, column inches were dedicated to the Aberdeen born centre-half. "Buchan - revelling in his new responsibility as skipper - must stay a fixture in the national team," wrote journalist Ian Cameron, who also reserved special praise for one of Buchan's compatriots. "Macari, beavering away in his recently adopted midfield role, could be poised for a spectacular comeback (to the Scotland team)."

Meanwhile, Willie Morgan was substituted - but this time, to no controversy, as he was the victim of a bad foul by Ken Knighton. It was an isolated incident in a game that Docherty felt had been fairly competed. "At least they came to play football instead of trying to kick us off the park, as others have done this season," he quipped. Journalist Douglas Peacock was less impressed. "Though they may not be marking time until their almost inevitable return to the First Division, Manchester United seem to have become bored by the flimsy challenge posed by such clubs as Sheffield Wednesday. They have shown often enough that they can rise to an occasion but if the occasion itself does not arise, they are apt to be as ordinary as the next team," wrote Peacock. Some readers may consider that statement to be as true today as it was when it was written, although to be fair, this can be a problem that inflicts many big clubs renowned for exciting football.

The reward for the (mostly) exciting football United had played in the League so far was now an extremely promising five point gap at the top ahead of Sunderland, who just so happened to be the Reds' next league opponents. Before that, was the chance of another reward, this time for the exciting football that had put a number of First Division clubs to the sword. Third placed Norwich City stood in the way of United and a Wembley final in the League Cup.

"Now we get down to the game that could be the gilt on the ginger bread!" wrote Docherty in *United Review* ahead of the game. "It's a tremendous feeling to consider that we are just one round short of playing in a Cup Final at Wembley. And it would indeed be a tremendous thrill if we could come out on top against Norwich City in this two-legged semi-final of the League Cup. Given a choice I would still opt for promotion back to the First Division in preference to honours in a Cup competition... my lads will be particularly keen to do well this evening after our brief appearance in the FA Cup... Norwich are chasing our leadership of the division very strongly and they gave us a glimpse of their abilities at Carrow Road earlier in the season by beating us 2-0. So we must not take anything for granted and it will call for a big effort in both legs if we are to succeed." Docherty also addressed the fact that the club now had a free weekend on which they might have been playing an F.A. Cup tie. "As it is, we now have a free Saturday on January 25, the date of the fourth round. Manchester City invited us to play a friendly, but I turned it down because I want to take advantage of the break that has come our way. By the time we come back next week after the semi-final second leg at Norwich the lads will be ready for a rest and I plan to give them a few days off. I just hope it will be a little celebration holiday rather than a rest to lick our wounds!"

WEDNESDAY 15TH JANUARY - LEAGUE CUP SEMI FINAL 1ST LEG
OLD TRAFFORD (58,010)

MANCHESTER UNITED 2-2 NORWICH CITY

Stepney, Forsyth, Houston, Greenhoff, James, Buchan, Morgan, McIlroy, Daly, Macari[2], McCalliog
Sub : Young

A bumper crowd were given a treat, despite watching this match in the pouring Manchester rain. The effect of the weather on the pitch made it evident that it wasn't just the players at Old Trafford who could do with a break. Not that there was any sign of tired legs in the opening stages; United came out of the blocks with the intention of putting the tie to bed early, missing great opportunities through Morgan, Macari and Greenhoff.

As often happens, the team that dominated the first half were caught out just before the break. "After pressing Norwich hard in the first half and failing to profit from the splendid flank service from Willie Morgan and Alex Forsyth, United suffered a sickening counter-punch blow a minute before the interval," reported Ronald Crowther. Norwich winger Powell gave the Canaries a half-time lead.

Half-time was most certainly welcomed by United, giving Docherty an opportunity to ensure his team weren't deflated by the untimely setback. He shifted formation, moving Greenhoff into midfield and putting Macari up front. While not exactly changing the game (United were certainly deserving of being level, if not in front), the switch paid instant dividends. Within 6 minutes of the restart, United were level - a corner was only half cleared to Greenhoff, whose cross was finished by a hooked bicycle kick from Macari, who must have had McIlroy's effort in a similar position from the weekend on his mind. After more pressure, it was another moment of magic from Macari that put the Reds in front - the little Scot received a cross from Houston on the edge of the six yard box, cleverly juggled the ball into a favourable position and then slammed it home from an unfavourable angle. "It seemed as though this would open the floodgates and indeed the Reds should have gone further in front when Willie Morgan was put clean through by Macari," described the club's official newsletter, "But Willie decided to try for a penalty instead of having a crack at goal and Referee Kew would have none of it."

The visitors still had a sting in their tail, however, with a familiar face returning to exact even more revenge. Ted MacDougall - scourge of the Reds back at Carrow Road - seized upon a back-pass from Greenhoff that held up on the muddy pitch (earlier in the pitch, the slow pitch had also denied Greenhoff a goal), evaded a challenge from the approaching Stepney and then, as described by Crowther, "contemptuously side-footed (the ball) into the net."

It was a body blow for the Reds who had put on their best show for weeks, but with no remaining League game bigger than the one coming up, there was no time for the players to be feeling sorry for themselves. At least in Macari's case, he was able to reflect on another big game performance. "I was very pleased of course, it's just so disappointing that there's no footage of it – particularly my goal against Norwich, which was one of my best!" says Macari. "It's especially annoying because believe it or not, the other leg of the semi final – Aston Villa and Chester City – was on television instead! That took priority – that's right, my best ever goal lost to Chester City! That's no good, is it?! Manchester United didn't dictate the television schedule back then – you can't imagine them not getting on TV because of Chester these days can you? I also scored a similar goal a few years later at Goodison on Boxing Day, but no footage of that exists either."

Macari's mixed form of 1973/74 was now improving with the player becoming increasingly important, though the man himself feels that he had nothing to prove. "I suppose some will look at that season and say that is when I found my feet but I felt I'd already proven myself at Celtic anyway," he says. "Perhaps it's more accurate to acknowledge that I was one of a number of players who were coming into a new team that the Doc was building – there was a natural struggle at the start as we all coped with the change, but the confidence that came with winning games helped us all."

Another injury to Pearson had ruled him out of the Norwich game. Instead of turning to Ron Davies, or perhaps using Macari as a temporary striker given his experience and brace against Norwich, Tommy Docherty dipped into the transfer market again, this time to make a short term loan signing for Tommy Baldwin of Chelsea. Docherty had managed Baldwin in his time at Stamford Bridge so the move made sense in that respect, if none other. Baldwin registered 73 goals in 183 league games for Chelsea – hardly prolific, but respectable enough, and no team was likely to be open to the idea of allowing someone indispensable leave on a temporary basis. However strange the move, Baldwin was in the number nine shirt for United's game at Roker Park.

SUNDERLAND 0-0 MANCHESTER UNITED

Stepney, Forsyth, Houston, Greenhoff, James, Buchan, Morgan, McIlroy, Baldwin, Macari, McCalliog

Prior to this head to head, Sunderland had had a game in hand for a while, but in the week before, they had played Southampton and only managed a draw – so, with 26 games played, United had 39 points to Sunderland's 34. Both sides were unbeaten at home and Sunderland's defensive record at home was even meaner, with just three goals conceded in twelve games. With a five-point gap of their own ahead of West Bromwich Albion in fifth (and three ahead of Norwich in the third and final promotion push)  both clubs had reason to think that victory in this game would give them a major boost in their search of promotion.

In the *Roker Review* for the game, the Journal's Kevin Francis wrote, "The tendency to count point-producing chickens before they hatch can indeed be a fatal past-time. The game contains far too many pitfalls for anyone to gaze into the future with any degree of confidence. But occasionally a situation arises in which uncertainties are slightly erased and supporters can glance with just a shade more optimism around the corner that leads to success or failure. And that, I feel, is the situation which fans of Manchester United and Sunderland now find themselves."

Prior to the game, Sunderland boss Bob Stokoe was presented with a gallon bottle of Bell's Whisky to mark his manager of the month award. After the champagne football served up by both sides in the November encounter, it would have been reasonable to expect something to whet the appetite this time around too. Why not? After all, these were the top two teams in the Division, and the top scorers to boot (Sunderland, at this point, had scored a goal more than United). Once again roared on by a highest attendance of the season for the team they were visiting, United and their hosts had all the motivation they needed to serve up another classic.

So, of course, it finished 0-0 – a result that would turn out to be far better for the momentum of the visitors, and damaging to that of the home team. That is not to say that the game wasn't without incident and quality. In fact, one of United's most experienced players would, many years later, refer to this as his favourite match – and the identity may leave you surprised!

Manchester United as a club is so decorated with legends that the five statues they currently have outside the club as of 2015 – not to mention the statue of Denis Law inside the Stretford End – could just as well be fifteen. Many debates are held about the respective qualities of the three teams that have won the European Cup for the club and also the lost potential of the 1958 side as well as the lost potential of this very side we are discussing that Docherty was putting together in 1974. Each player has played their part and rightfully claimed their place in history but it goes without saying that the goalscorers are always remembered.

Once the goals are accounted for, the events of the respective encounters are replayed, and it's a fair shout to say that Alex Stepney's save at the end of the 1968 European Cup Final from Eusebio's rasping drive is the most important in the club's history. Eusebio's shot was relatively kind for Stepney in that it required strength and sensibility rather than movement to stop it from going past him, but many goalkeepers have failed to stop similar efforts, and strength and sensibility were just about Stepney's biggest strengths. Without that save, there would have been no extra time at Wembley, and no fulfilment of Sir Matt Busby's dream. No romantic conclusion to the tragic story of Munich. The club would have come so close, but ultimately failed, and from that moment on, although the recovery of Manchester United as a club and a team to achieve what they had from Munich until that moment was certainly far more than just a commendable accomplishment, it would not be quite so revered. Stepney shrugs it off, but his mere presence and capability to hold on to the ball when it must have carried one hell of a sting (because there was no way that Eusebio would miss a rebound) did not just influence a result or the destiny of a trophy, it influenced an identity.

Even if humbly disregarding the profound importance of what it meant, one would assume that such a moment would stand out for any player as their career highlight. But for Alex Stepney, it is the impassioned, intimidating Roker Roar in 1974 that played host to his favourite ever game, and not the bright lights of Wembley 1968. "Roker Park is a tremendous ground to play on. There was a packed crowd and the BBC covered it for Match Of The Day – a then Second Division match, remember," recalls Stepney. "Luckily, crowds have never affected me, you just dare not let it happen! Sunderland had played us at Old Trafford a couple of months earlier, losing a great game 3-2, so they were after revenge. With their fanatical crowd behind them the early stages were always going to be vital, and from a goalkeeper's point of view, busy. It was, but it lasted the whole match! It turned out to be my best ever performance… everything I did came off. It started when Billy Hughes turned quickly in our area and hit a shot which my outstretched fingertips turned onto a post, luckily the ball came back to me, not Billy! Our midfield was becoming so overworked that the forwards were being constantly pulled back, our penalty area being like Piccadilly Circus at times. Probably my best save came right on half time when Tony Towers, the former Manchester City player, cracked a vicious shot from about twenty yards, which with the area being as crowded left me unsighted until the last second when I just took off and managed to hang onto the ball. Martin Buchan was a tower of strength, not only in this particular match, but during the time we played together. A marvellous reader of the game, really a player in the Bobby Moore class in that position. Despite the pounding we took, our defensive play enabled us to draw this match 0-0, giving us another vital point."

However difficult it is to compare the context, from a professional logic, it does make sense that a clean sheet and what he considers to be his best ever performance would register at the top of his list. What is a good match for a goalkeeper and a defender is not necessarily the best spectacle for most supporters although most still appreciate that not every game can be won and sometimes it is those at the back that come out of some games with the most credit. For United supporter Gary Thompson, Stepney's performance was particularly noteworthy. "The best performance during the '74/75 season ironically wasn't from one of my favourites - Greenhoff, Daly or McIlroy - but Alex Stepney in the away game at Sunderland. He saved everything that came his way," says Gary. The definition of what makes a good match is purely subjective, but one thing Manchester United supporters could commonly agree on was that the draw was a fine result in the pursuit of their primary objective.

"United gave their chances of returning to the top grade as Second Division champions a tremendous boost with this hard earned point against Sunderland at Roker Park," postulated edition four of the club's official newsletter, "For not only did this drawn game leave the Reds five points clear of the Wearsiders, but it also gave them a ten point lead over the teams who are outside the promotion zone." The newsletter conceded that it was far from a spectacle. "In a match that was a complete contrast to the one played at Old Trafford between the clubs in November, United found themselves constantly on the defensive as Sunderland fought to close the championship gap. Alex Stepney was in, what can only be described as, incredible form, for he pulled off saves that he had no right to. Finney, Robson, Malone, Watson, Kerr, yes practically all the Sunderland team had efforts foiled by Alex. United made only one change from the midweek side that played against Norwich City, newly loaned Tommy Baldwin coming in for Gerry Daly who moved to substitute, and it would be unfair to judge Tommy on this outing as it was not United's day in the attacking department. Martin Buchan and Steve James were outstanding in a defence that grew in confidence as the game progressed."

On the same theme as Stepney, Buchan had great memories of the times United came up against Sunderland. "I really enjoyed playing against Sunderland because they were always good games and great occasions," he says. "I was good friends with Billy Hughes and Bobby Kerr, and would go out with them quite often after midweek matches. I used to love playing at Roker Park because the atmosphere was simply incredible."

It was a defensive resilience that the Reds would have to count on again as they prepared for the second leg of their League Cup semi final. The free weekend created by elimination in the FA Cup meant there was a space of nine days between the return against Norwich City and United's next league game against Bristol City at Old Trafford. For all the talk about tiredness and fixture congestion, there could be no excuse for Docherty's men not leaving everything out on the pitch.

Norwich, of course, were involved in the Division Two promotion push themselves but had dropped points against York City on the same day of the Sunderland/United draw, meaning a missed opportunity to close the gap on second place. Without wishing to give too much away in terms of spoilers for the season, following the draw at Roker Park, Sunderland stuttered, picking up just sixteen points from their last fifteen games (30 points were available). They finished in fourth, a bitterly disappointing end to a season that had started so promisingly.

By contrast, it was Norwich City manager John Bond who seemed thoroughly depressed in his programme notes ahead of the second leg. "I can only guess what our supporters were feeling after last Saturday's match here with York. And if, like me, they were all sick as pigs, then who could blame them?" he lamented, later saying, "My objective this season is to get Norwich City back into the First Division. That takes priority over everything else. And if we fail, I fail... and it adds up to another big let-down to you good folk who, as I have already said, have given us some truly magnificent support this season. When you look at our recent League record... well, the less said, really, the better. I think we have taken something like ten points from a possible 26. And that's not promotion form. It has more of a hint of relegations about it than anything else... Going back to that York match, I have often said that the main problem in a game like this, coming so close to that first leg League Cup semi-final at Manchester on the Wednesday night, is one of motivation and getting the players back in tune for a completely different sort of game with a completely different sort of atmosphere."

Bond's comments provide an interesting context for Tommy Docherty's thoughts throughout the season. Both were focussed on promotion but even a club of Norwich's stature believed that they found it difficult to motivate themselves for the hum-drum of - with all due respect - lower quality opposition. When Norwich City were failing to get excited for the task of York City at home, it provides some sort of perspective to the enormity with which people viewed United being in the second tier. It also provides the perspective about the importance of promotion against success in the League Cup – Bond was unashamedly as open as Docherty when it came to his preference.

Elsewhere in the programme, the 'Canaries' Forum' featured contributions from supporters who also seemed more concerned with the mathematic permutations of the League than the possible trip to Wembley which awaited the victors of the evenings game. P.B. Woodward wrote, "Can you tell me how the goal average system works. I always like to work out City's League position, but I am stuck where goal average is concerned. I am sure many other supporters have the same problem." Ken Brown, the assistant manager at the club, replied, "This is not so difficult as it sounds… you divide the "goals for" into the "goals against." At face value it seems understandable that lower division clubs would prioritise promotion over Cup success but in this situation, the team awaiting the victors of this semi final were either Second Division Aston Villa or Fourth Division promotion chasers Chester City, who had drawn 2-2 in the first leg. United's illustrious list of victims in the competition meant they should surely have felt confident coming up against anyone, and with the carrot of European football on offer, it is illogical to the point of it being unreasonable to suggest that United would do anything but go hell for leather. From the point of view of the travelling supporters, the opportunity for a first Wembley appearance – and Cup success – in seven years was probably as exciting, if not possibly moreso, than the expected promotion from the Second Division. It would certainly go some way to explaining the events of the 22nd January.

That said, there was an interesting subplot that could also have said to be inciting. The day before the game, United's team coach was targeted by criminals who tampered with the bus by hammering a nail through the clutch pipe. On Wednesday, the tap on the pressure tank was opened, causing a drain to stop the brakes working. Fortunately, the coach was tested before departure, and disaster was averted. The club informed the police, who declared that there was 'no real damage' and that it was 'an incident, not a crime', which angered United manager Tommy Docherty. "If this had happened to the Prime Minister's car, police would have been swarming all over the place. Does somebody have to get killed before action is taken?" he raged. It was an unwanted subplot that interrupted preparations for the game, and it is a possibility that the long night's sleep that awaited United's coaching staff (Docherty said that he, coach Tommy Cavanagh, physio Laurie Brown and coach driver Howard Wilson would take turns to 'watch' the bus in the depot overnight) was on the manager's mind at Carrow Road.

WEDNESDAY 22ND JANUARY - LEAGUE CUP SEMI FINAL SECOND LEG
CARROW ROAD (31,621)

NORWICH CITY 1-0 MANCHESTER UNITED

Stepney, Forsyth, Houston, Greenhoff, James, Buchan, Morgan, McIlroy, Daly, Macari, McCalliog

Sub : Young

Colin Suggett was the man responsible for United's premature departure from the League Cup, but as far as the Reds were concerned, everyone in a yellow shirt was a villain. "The raw hunger of the teams for the massive bonus waiting for whoever reached Wembley added ferocity to the second leg of this semi-final," read one report, "The tackling began at the knee-caps and worked progressively higher until Duncan Forbes was booked for the last of a grim success of fouls on Lou Macari which were threatening to decapitate the little Scot who scored United's two first leg goals." United, possibly exhausted from the provocation, responded in kind. "Alex Forsyth sought a remedy in a lunge at Ted MacDougall which might have killed his former team-mate if it had landed."

Suggett's goal was a scrambled effort early in the second half, a strike worthy of settling this match given the scrappiness into which it descended. Still, if Docherty's men were attempting to settle the score figuratively, they were also doing so literally, and were arguably the better side. Macari, United's first leg hero, was the star man for the visitors, but was unable to inspire any opportunities of note against a resolute and aggressive Norwich City rearguard. With around ten minutes left, Sammy McIlroy's header was well saved – United's best, and only, opportunity worthy of note in the closing stages. Willie Morgan later claimed that after the game, as the players were heading into the dressing room, Docherty shook their hands one by one, except for Morgan's.

Almost predictably, the violent undertones of the match led to violence in Norwich afterwards – though that is not to say that predictable means understandable. "Ten people were arrested last night in Norwich when Soccer fans went on the rampage after Norwich City beat Manchester United," read one report, while another was far more specific.

"Close Old Trafford, MP Urges" reported the *Daily Telegraph*, with the finger pointed squarely at United followers once more. "The Minister for Sport, Mr Howell, is to be asked by Mr William Wilson, Labour MP for Coventry SE to close Old Trafford football ground as a punishment for Manchester United supporters who went on the rampage in Norwich in Wednesday... Manchester fans smashed windows and overturned cars. Ten arrests were made. Mr Wilson, himself a soccer supporter, is seeing Mr Howell to demand the closure of the ground because 'any real supporter is sick and tired of their fans' behaviour.' He said the Football League had done little more than 'wring their hands' and say: 'Behave yourselves' after a succession of assaults and vandalism by United supporters. It was 'time for drastic action'. In September, after United drew with West Bromwich Albion and their supporters were fined for offences concerned with breaches of the peace, a senior police officer described United's fans as 'the scum of the hooligans of this country.'"

Today, Sammy McIlroy looks back on those kind of comments with annoyance. "Away from home it was pretty bad and the press really built it up," he admits. "We'd travel by train quite often on the same trains as fans and we'd see trouble, and the police in their hordes directing them. The press made a meal of it because it was United but the hooligan element was all over the sport. It was news and it was made the most of. The clubs couldn't believe that United supporters would turn up in the numbers they did. We broke records wherever we went... it felt like a home game for us because we had as many fans as the home team. We'd see shop windows, shops, cars smashed and you'd think 'Bloody hell'... you know, we didn't like it, but we didn't want the supporters to stop coming because by and large it was always great."

However, McIlroy was more upset about the League Cup exit – a result that still grates with him to this day.

"I was so gutted. Absolutely gutted," he confesses. "I think, to be fair, we lost it in the first leg. After the second leg it was the lowest I'd felt for a long time. Even though Norwich were a good, experienced team and had MacDougall who seemed to score against us all the time, we were so much better in both games. To see them celebrating that they were going to Wembley was so disappointing. To lose in a semi-final can be worse than losing a final. At least getting to a final you get the build up, get to play there, but to be so close and lose out on that was a horrible feeling. I got on well with Ted but him scoring was still salt in the wound; it was probably more aggravating for the Doc. Even more so because if we had won a trophy, and got into Europe, relegation would have been completely forgotten about."

Still, the Cup run did have its benefits. "It didn't matter who we played, whether it was First or Second Division sides, we just felt so confident of winning, especially at home," says McIlroy. "Of course those wins added to our confidence... winning breeds confidence, simple as that, and we couldn't wait for the next game."

There were nine days until he would see his team play again but there was never going to be a full week pass without Docherty hitting the headlines and when Scotland manager Willie Ormond left out the in-form Lou Macari, the United boss was incredulous. "He (Macari) is entitled to be sick. He's playing out of his skin, better than at any time of his life, and he's good for years. I'm only surprised Scotland haven't gone for Celtic's Billy McNeil, who's pushing 40, and how about my assistant manager Paddy Crerand, who's older than I am?!" Docherty quipped. Although clearly a joke – Crerand is much younger than Docherty – it was the kind of comment hardly likely to endear Crerand to his boss.

Recollections of the trio would have this period as the time that Morgan and Crerand began to fall out with the manager, or, depending on how you perceive it, the manager found the pair dispensable and begun to plan for life without them. Was that because Docherty, filled with the confidence of seeing his United team doing and playing well, finally felt secure enough in his position to exert his authority?

FEBRUARY

PERHAPS HE WAS TIRED of talking about it, but for whatever reason, Docherty neglected to comment on the crowd trouble that followed the Norwich game, the automobile trouble that preceded it, or Macari's Scotland exclusion when compiling his notes for the next match programme, the home game against Bristol City.

"So near yet so far! That is how Wembley looks now after going down to Norwich City in the semi-final of the League Cup," he said. "I felt very disappointed for the players after our 1-0 defeat at Carrow Road and sorry for you supporters as well. The team had worked hard and like you had come to fancy a trip to Wembley. You, the fans, had also played your part with your tremendous support and I know you must have shared the feeling of anti-climax. But this is something that we must put behind us right away as we welcome Bristol City to Old Trafford to pick up our league programme again. This can still be a fantastic season for Manchester United if we finish off the job we have started so well and clinch a return to the First Division at the first attempt. As I have stressed all along, promotion is the priority this year and I would not like to see disappointment in the Cup take any steam out of our campaign in the Second Division. It was hard trying to get the players out of their depression immediately after the Norwich match, but as I tried to point out to them, they had in fact done well… the players did everything I asked of them, but in the Cup you have got to have the breaks. It went for Norwich that night, not that I am complaining because we had our breaks to reach the semi-final. So good luck to Norwich. We are a young side and will learn from the experience. This is not the end but the beginning of a new drive to win the Second Division championship. With the right attitude I am even more confident that we shall pull it off. There is nothing to distract us… With our lead at the top of the Second Division I think we could have managed to go for the double, but now there are no doubts. We can concentrate on our remaining League fixtures and make sure we build on that good result we had at Roker Park.

"Sunderland are the best team we have played in the Second Division and to take three points from them is some achievement… what we must now do is make sure that we do not waste those valuable points picked up from Sunderland. I gave the lads a break over last weekend to bring them back fresh for this afternoon's match with this in mind. Bristol City are an improving side and are right on the brink of a promotion place. You can be sure that they will be full of football action today and we shall have to be on our toes to fulfil our championship ambitions… especially without the Cup to distract us!"

SATURDAY 1ST FEBRUARY - DIVISION TWO - OLD TRAFFORD (47,117)

MANCHESTER UNITED 0-1 BRISTOL CITY

Stepney, Forsyth, Houston, Daly (Young), James, Buchan, Morgan, McIlroy, Baldwin, Macari, McCalliog

After United not only failed to score again, but fell to a late, late goal chasing victory against Bristol City, one report read, "Champions, even aspiring champions, should never lead with their chin… that Don Gillies goal, scored with the last kick of the game, was the most blatant example of United's tactical immaturity."

In reference to a bomb scare that threatened to halt proceedings in the 35th minute, journalist Martin Leach's report came with the headline, "Bristol bombers spot on". The PA system relayed

Sammy McIlroy wins a header against Bristol City

information that they had received a phone call saying a bomb had been planted in the Stretford End, and that the game would go on but the gates would be opened if people wished to leave. The Stretford End replied in unison – 'We shall not be moved'. "It (the late winner) was an injustice, but United could not complain having failed with better chances and failing to make the most of enormous pressure, particularly in the second half," Leach wrote. "But until City's stunning winner, this was a match of a million yawns for United's one millionth customer of the season. It even took a bomb warning to move the Stretford enders to enthusiasm for an affair which was as dreary as the Second Division too often produces."

Macari's goals against Norwich City had taken him to twelve for the season, level with the still injured Stuart Pearson, but neither he or Pearson's stand in, Tommy Baldwin, could break down the Bristol defence. Steve James came closest with a thunderous 30 yard effort which smashed against the visitors crossbar yet despite not having much joy in creating good opportunities, United pushed forward in their hordes late on to try and make up for the disappointment of missing out on Wembley and get the League campaign back on track. In the closing stages, James had an effort blocked on the line, and struck the rebounding ball back towards goal – it was once again blocked on the line, before City broke through Keith Fear. Fear's run took him all the way to United's touchline, and he pulled the ball back for Gillies to easily finish.

"Even sitting on the bench, I could smell that goal coming," said Docherty afterwards. "They should have got the scent of it too. They should have decided among themselves on the field in those last ten minutes that they had worked hard to earn a point. They should have chosen to hold onto that instead of going forward to try and get a winner. That's what Leeds and Liverpool, the really top professional sides, would have done. The trouble is that there is not enough talking among our players on the field. They do all their talking in the bath afterwards, when it's too late. One problem of course is that the Old Trafford crowd keep urging them on to attack and the players tend to respond without making sure it's safe. Well they've paid for it… I suppose it's all part of a team growing up."

That, of course, is a rational explanation. It still seemed like a harsh lesson or review of a team that was missing Greenhoff, Holton, and Pearson, three crucial members of the spine of the team – the latter two had been missing for the majority of a run of just one win in eight matches. Surprisingly, defeat to Bristol City – who incidentally, in victory, completed a famous league 'double' over their illustrious opponents – had no impact on United's league position. Five points clear at the top, they were never going to drop down a place whatever the result, but Sunderland also lost, meaning the five point gap between the clubs remained in place.

Harsh it may have been but Docherty was convinced that recent results were down to under-performance of his players as much as the missing qualities of the list of absentees. And so with a trip to Oxford United – who his team had crushed 4-0 at Old Trafford – up next, and despite being able to select Greenhoff and Pearson once more, Docherty made his boldest move yet, replacing Alex Stepney (who, lest we forget, had just played one of the best games of his career) with 24 year-old Paddy Roche, who was making his Manchester United debut. It may be worth looking a little deeper into Docherty's words to understand his frustration – it is interesting that when analysing his team's performance, he was not comparing it to the standard set by the rest of the Division, rather, the best teams in the country. With that in mind, it's more understandable, even though Stepney's omission was still rather surprising.

The season had worn on long enough by this point, particularly with clubs now having determined their own objectives for the final run in, to render the novelty of Manchester United coming to town as a subplot to their main cause. Oxford were in 8th, four points off Norwich City in third – maybe an unrealistic target to catch, but with 13 games remaining, surely an objective great enough to at least aspire to.

SATURDAY 8TH FEBRUARY - DIVISION TWO - MANOR GROUND (15,815)

OXFORD UNITED 1-0 MANCHESTER UNITED

Stepney, Forsyth, Houston, Greenhoff, James, Buchan, Morgan, McIlroy, Pearson, Macari (Davies), McCalliog

With twenty-two teams in the division and only three of those getting promotion, some teams have to be realistic, and Oxford manager Gerry Summers certainly was in his programme notes. "The game is all about scoring goals, you win championships by putting a reasonable amount of chances away... our goal record speaks for itself, we lack guts and determination in the penalty box. If you look at the top of the Second Division you realise what might have been if our away record had been slightly better," he said. He had a point – Oxford had eleven wins at home, as many as United, but only one win from fifteen away games. Only Oldham and Millwall had failed to win away from home.

After the trouble that had plagued United throughout the season and as recently as their last away game, any trepidation among the hosts in terms of what kind of trouble they might be expecting would have been understandable. David Meek wrote a few words for the Oxford programme, saying "United have been delighted with the plans to welcome their fans at Oxford. They have become more used to terms like 'red menace' than talk of a red carpet for their arrival, and it has been a welcome change."

That welcome was clear as supporters entered the stadium, with a huge sign on one of the stands that read "WELCOME THE REDS". As always, the hospitable welcome didn't quite extend to on-pitch generosity with some miserly defending. For all of Summers' concerns about his own team's failures in front of goal, Docherty was now witnessing his once free-scoring men go a fourth consecutive game without a goal.

Just as against Bristol City, United had multiple attempts blocked on the goal line by desperate defenders – even though Oxford's goal was against the run of play when it came in the 35th minute, it was a goal worthy of deciding any game. Derek Clarke managed the rare feat of tricking Martin Buchan on the edge of the box and then unleashed an effort that beat Roche and struck the inside of the post on its way in.

United's search for an equaliser meant the withdrawal, once more, of Morgan for Davies, and even though Macari again was orchestrating play well from midfield, the visitors were simply incapable of finding the net. "Indeed, the game was a bit of an anti-climax," reported journalist Bill Meredith. "For all their pressure, though, United rarely showed the smooth precision of promotion candidates. They seemed to lack confidence; to pass across the pitch instead of making incisive thrusts into the heart of Oxford's defence." It was a story all too familiar with United supporters for whom the memories of the consequence of what happens to a goal shy team were painfully fresh.

Reporter John Parsons concurred with Meredith. "Roy Burton, the often besieged Oxford goalkeeper, produced a starring role for television," wrote Parsons, referring to the fact that once more, United were being shown on Match of the Day. Parsons also referred to a metal bar and a gin bottle being thrown into the goalmouth, apparently by away fans. "More than 200 Manchester United fans ran riot and spurned Oxford's 'let's be friends' approach this afternoon. The teenagers tried to smash down gates and get into the Manor ground when they couldn't buy tickets... Earlier, an Oxford United director, Dave Meeson, a former Reading goalkeeper, was assaulted by a group of youngsters. He was not seriously hurt," read one local report. "All this was a slap in the face for the joint trouble-avoiding moves of Manchester United and Oxford United. The elaborate 'peace' plans started yesterday when Reds director Sir Matt Busby opened a new section of the Oxford ground."

United had struggled to maintain much of the early buzz, but Sammy McIlroy later attributed that to the logic that most teams go through a seasonal dip. "We did suffer aggressive tactics against us but we couldn't keep up the pace we had for 9 months," he says. "All teams go through a dip and the manager and Tommy Cavanagh were warning us that it would. We were a little bit disappointed with ourselves but we had set the standard and built a lead, and when we looked at the table we looked at the likes of Villa and Norwich and knew that they would have their own blips as well. We knew we could turn it around and it became more about the response, rediscovering the form which had really started well."

Docherty had been keen to paint the recent drab form as a learning curve for his young team which was understandable considering it was only recently he had rediscovered the confidence within himself to be the successful manager of Manchester United that he had so believed when he first walked into the job. After this latest poor result he insisted 'we had better chances than we had when we beat them 4-0 at Old Trafford'. Actions speak louder than words and the identity of United's next opponents at least ensured the players would be ready for the fight.

SATURDAY 15TH FEBRUARY - DIVISION TWO - OLD TRAFFORD (44,712)

MANCHESTER UNITED 2-0 HULL CITY

Roche, Forsyth, Houston[1], Greenhoff, James (Davies), Buchan, Morgan, McIlroy, Pearson[1], Macari, Martin

"It's nice to be at the top of the table… but there are snags! For one thing everyone wants to take an extra hard swipe at you and knock you off your perch. This is especially true if you are Manchester United," wrote Docherty in *United Review*, perhaps as a reminder to everyone including his own players. "I have mentioned before a great many teams raise their game against us to such an extent that they seem spent for their next few matches. However I am not complaining about that. I

would rather be at the top and be swiped at than merely one of the challengers trying to do the swiping. Manchester United have also come to live with the fact that opposing sides try hard to beat us. This happens to all successful clubs and I am just happy to be in that elite bracket. What sometimes does make me a little mad is the way the spotlight tries to expose and exaggerate chinks in the armour of a team enjoying a prominent place.

"Manchester United for instance are going through a spell at the moment which has lost us a few points. Compared with our progress in the first half of the season we would appear to have lost our touch. But is it really fair to expect a team to win practically every match? Even the really great sides like Leeds United of a few seasons ago eventually lose and there was no way we could have continued right through the season as we did for the first four months... I was naturally disappointed to lose at Oxford, but I refuse to join the people in the various media who seem to think that we are a spent force. What is happening is the kind of spell which happens to everyone at some stage or other. We are not scoring goals but I am confident this will change because we are doing all the other right things. Defensively we are still tight – no-one has hammered us during our little off-spell and all the missed points have been by a single goal. We are also moving quite well in midfield and in most games we have had two-thirds of the play. We have created the scoring chances as well. In other words we have done everything but score."

There was plenty of motivation – it was the day after Valentine's Day but there was no love lost between the sides following their bruising encounter at Boothferry Park in November, which, as we remember, Docherty described as the 'most brutal in five years'. United's last home game had seen the club suffer the ignominy of being 'doubled' by Bristol City and with all their recent frustrations in mind perhaps it was predictable that they would begin quickly.

It took just ninety seconds for all United's recent troubles in front of goal to be forgotten. Alex Forsyth's free kick was met by Stewart Houston - his first effort was blocked by Hull defender Dave Roberts, but Houston was able to convert the rebound. It was hard luck for Roberts who was actually making his 'Tigers' debut – he was part of the Oxford defence that had kept United out the previous week!

Roberts had clearly settled into life fairly quickly – as like in the first game between the sides, Hull were uncompromising to put it kindly. The new Hull defender was giving Pearson a rough time, but it was visiting defender Steve Deere who was booked for a foul on the former Hull man, shortly after Chris Galvin had been booked for bringing down McIlroy with force. The tough tackling seemingly had an effect on United's confidence in playing their natural game. As Bert Thorpe reported, "Things cooled after that [Deere's booking] but the game generally was below standard. There were too many negative passing movements and too few players willing to try the unorthodox." However, the visitors had not account for the bravery of McIlroy. He stood up to the roughhouse tactics, was booked for a retaliatory challenge on Deere, but most important he continued to attempt to beat his marker.

It was that bravery from McIlroy which made the difference but not before Hull had claimed a victim – Steve James was stretchered off with suspected damaged ankle ligaments. Ron Davies came on and was involved in the move that secured the points for United, just before half time. "McIlroy and Alex Forysth exchanged passes near the corner flag and when the Irishman centred Davies rose high to head the ball back for Pearson to hook powerfully into the net," wrote Thorpe. "The slide has been halted, but the early season glitter has a dulled edge. And before Manchester United can be hailed as Second Division champions I will want more evidence of a return to consistency," he had opened his report with.

United's next league game was at League Cup finalists Aston Villa, by far the toughest fixture remaining on paper. Norwich

City - who had been the scourge of the Reds so far - were still to visit Old Trafford, but with that being a home game, the chances were at least in United's favour.

It may be straying from the topic somewhat but the near future of Villa (and, to be completely accurate, Nottingham Forest, too) represents what Manchester United might well feel they could have been challenging for if things had continued on their natural path. Villa would go from the Second Division in 1975 to First Division Champions in 1981, and European Champions in 1982. Nottingham Forest - 12th in Division Two on the morning of February 22nd, 1975, would taste success even sooner, winning the First Division in 1978 (the year after Docherty was sacked) and the European Cup in 1979 and 1980. This of course proves nothing about the potential of Docherty and United but it underlines two things - first, that anything was possible, so talk of the potential of this team should not be dismissed as folly. Brian Greenhoff and Gordon Hill would later go on record as saying they were only a Peter Shilton-type in goal from winning the League and European Cup. Docherty had attempted to sign Shilton in 1974 but in 1977 he was signed by Forest instead.

The second thing it underlines is the competitiveness in British football at the time, and how strong an era it was for the English league (which perhaps makes it all the more staggering that the country didn't qualify for the 1978 World Cup).

"In today's game those that have money can go and win something and succeed. Back in those days teams like Nottingham Forest and Derby County could spend just as much and more than Manchester United. So instead of two or three teams challenging, it was nine or ten. It was like that down the divisions too," says Lou Macari. "You can see just how good the teams were by the European record over the 70's and 80's."

In February 1975, as he prepared to see his team take on

Manchester United, Ron Saunders was showing the kind of attitude that would see him take his club right to the pinnacle of the game. "Six or seven weeks ago everyone was saying that the outcome of the promotion race from the Second Division was a forgone (sic) conclusion with Manchester United to finish as Champions, Sunderland as Runners-up and Norwich City taking third place. I didn't share this view and went on record by saying so in this column," wrote Saunders in his match programme notes. "A glance at the League table shows that some peoples idea of a 'foregone conclusion' has now become a promotion contest which now involves nearly half the teams in the division and no-one is going to be able to relax in the slightest until the season is over and done with… so there will be a large number of clubs awaiting the outcome of our game with Manchester United today with great interest. It's a 'four pointer' in the fullest sense and both sides will be flat out to win."

It is worth pointing out that Villa, too, were a sleeping giant. This was their centenary year and their match programme pointed out that in that time they had achieved many 'firsts', and at the time were the most successful team in FA Cup history, having won the trophy seven times. Villa were, of course, preparing for the League Cup final the following week against Norwich at Wembley. Where Docherty had suggested the Cup exits might benefit his team in terms of concentration in the League (a hope, rather than a plan, and one that unfortunately hadn't come to fruition), Villa had seen the other side of the coin. That the momentum generated from a Cup run can inspire confidence in momentum all around.

If all this leads to a belief that Villa considered themselves at least equals to United at present, then their programme profile on United was generous if not starry-eyed. "Manchester United have brought glamour, glory and growth to the Second Division this season," it said. "The GLAMOUR of fielding no less than 13 full internationals in the League programme. The GLORY of leading the table from the first kick in August. And the GROWTH of pumping over £100,000 of extra cash into the pockets of their divisional partners after only two thirds of the season… visiting clubs have gleefully picked up an average of around £3,500 from a trip to Manchester. What better evidence to support the widely-held belief that Manchester United is still the most famous name in British football? Certainly, the Mancunian misery in the hour of relegation last year was shared by thousands of Continental followers who had admired Sir Matt Busby's team in the European Cup."

A 'Sunsport special' in the week before the game had corroborated those figures. "The city of Manchester houses more than half a million people. The United of Manchester has housed almost a million since last August. In stark figures, 971,932 fans have watched Manchester United's 21 matches at Old Trafford this season… On their travels, United have set the Second Division box offices alight. Nearly 400,000 have seen their 15 away League matches and in 13 of them they provided their hosts' biggest League "gate" of the season. On Saturday United will walk out at Villa Park before a 50,000 all-ticket crowd - double Villa's regular attendance."

SATURDAY 22ND FEBRUARY - DIVISION TWO
VILLA PARK (40,353)

ASTON VILLA 2-0 MANCHESTER UNITED

Stepney, Forsyth, Houston, Greenhoff, Sidebottom, Buchan, Morgan, McIlroy, Pearson, Macari, Martin (Davies)

50,000 may have been a bit of an over-estimate but 40,353 comfortably beat the previous highest league gate at Villa Park that season which had been 25,673 against Blackpool.

Docherty suggested before the game that Villa players would be playing for their Cup final places but gave no explanation for the return of Stepney (curious, as Roche had done nothing of blame in either the Oxford defeat or the win over Hill). Sidebottom came back in for the injured James while Mick Martin kept his place as the manager attempted to discover whether the 23 year-old had a future at United.

The visitors began well but by half time were trailing by two goals. Pearson mis-directed an interception and Villa got the ball into the box, engineering a move which Ray Graydon steered in. The veteran defender Charlie Aitken headed in a second as the hosts were rewarded for an enterprising first half display with both points. Though United weren't rewarded with any real opportunities to get back into the match as Villa played it safe in the second half, it wasn't for the want of trying from the excellent Macari who did more than anybody to make sure United's opponents were not given an easy ride. It wasn't enough to prevent the Reds slipping to their seventh League defeat of the season and their fourth in seven games. To his credit, Docherty had proven himself to be a very gracious loser throughout the season – that is, on the occasions when he felt that the opponents had played with the right spirit of the game. After seeing his team kicked, bruised and battered, and frustrated by teams in recent weeks, he could have no complaints about watching them beaten by the better team on the day. "Villa are in a successful patch at the moment. Many people would have thought that the week before playing at Wembley would have found them lacking in concentration. But concentration is just what they did have against us at Villa Park and with help of an early goal they gave us one of our few chasings," he said the following week. "No-one really tears us apart these days, but I must say Villa came the nearest...Villa in fact let us off the hook. The score could have been bigger against us."

With Saunders and Docherty, it was always likely that the post-match discussions would prove to be every bit as entertaining as the game itself.

"Docherty, having lost the match, came out to win the inquest," read one report. "He had just convinced us that United had performed a miracle to stay so far in front through a patch of bad results when Saunders walked in scowling: 'This is my room.' Docherty said: 'Well get the drinks out.'

"Saunders: "That was all you were ever going to get today. That referee used to live four doors from me.'

"Docherty: 'It didn't make any difference, the way we played. One of my players just tried to jump in the bath and fell out the window.'

"Saunders: 'But we pulled it off despite all those injuries.'

"Docherty: 'When I saw your lads going down with knocks I shouted to all four of them to come off and let us make a game of it'.

"Docherty - 'privately I'm sick as a parrot' - kept wisecracking and promised United would pull even further into the lead once the grounds dried out. Docherty was less kind towards his own team, labelling their performance 'lethargic', a 'disgrace', and 'like schoolboys'. United's poor form had also attracted the attention of reporters. One - Clive White - went even further and wrote that United "could be sent straight back down again" should they get promoted, noting that the team carried many of the characteristics of the side that were relegated the previous season - 'a dithering, sluggish defence, no brains in midfield, and no height in attack'.

Considering how the team and squad would pull together over the next few years it was a statement that showed gross misjudgement from White. Not necessarily on the Alan Hansen level but not far short. In fact, in nitpicking certain qualities which he perceived to be lacking, he could barely have been more mistaken. Martin Buchan would mature into one of the finest defenders in the clubs history, while the pocket-pinching midfield skills of Macari and McIlroy (coupled with their attacking invention) made them a combination revered for years to come. Did he have a point about their height up front? Pearson was as capable and renowned a finisher with his head as he was with his feet. United had struggled of late, that was a given and was very evident in their form, but the scathing attack was so hard that it almost appeared to be unreasonable. Had he named names, it may well have been libellous!

However, as far over the line those remarks were, what was certainly true was that United needed to buck up their ideas. White was maybe over-reacting to a run of games. It has to be said that only against Villa can United truly be said to not have had the lions share of the chances, but profligacy was still a problem that needed to be eradicated. Having attempted to address the reasons for his team's dropped points, Docherty may have been most accurate when he openly considered the impact of the winter weather on pitches, and subsequently, the way he liked his team to play.

Nonetheless, he read the riot act to his players in the week that followed, making a number of behind the scenes changes - telling them to mind what they said in the press and shy away from anything that might court controversy, and also telling them that they must stop going out so much in order to focus their concentration on promotion. The manager's recollection of an event at the start of this record where he confronted three players at a bar - Pearson, Macari, McCalliog- and the way things transpired, suggests it took place around this time. Given what was about to happen with the latter, it makes chronological sense.

Interestingly, Martin Buchan has a different take on the dip in form. Buchan may well have had an excuse for his own performance not being quite as effective as everyone at the club had become accustomed to because of the lack of a consistent partner. The centre half's contribution did not in fact diminish and his importance grew as the season wore on. Buchan does however believe that it was in the absence of Jim Holton that caused the temporary problem as the team adjusted. "Jim was a big miss," he says. "He was an ideal player to have in that division because you'd come up against a lot of teams who would be out to show the supposed United fancy dans a thing or two. Jim, a rugged centre half, was initially a big miss, and we adjusted eventually, but it was no coincidence that his absence was followed by our worst form of the season. I just did my best in the circumstances. I can still remember the tackle by Eric McMordie that saw Big Jim carried off. When I was playing alongside the shorter defenders, particularly Brian, we had to be very well organised. We were both five feet ten inches tall but in the main we got away with our lack of height. I would always say to Brian that we must keep the opposition centre forwards out of the box at all costs. If someone beats you in the air and scores with a header from 20 yards it's either a very, very good header or a steward's enquiry into the goalkeeper. If they get a flick on in the box around 3 or 4 yards out, the keeper's got no chance and as defenders you are responsible. I felt so sorry for Jim, because I'd played with him for Scotland as well as United. He had terrible luck, as proved by the injury he suffered against Red Star Belgrade before a friendly that ultimately cost him his career at Old Trafford."

Though not quite a consequence of underperformance in this bad run of form (he remained at Old Trafford for a few months into the following season) the Aston Villa match marked the end of Arnie Sidebottom's first team career at Manchester United. Arnie concedes that he found life hard in the uncompromising world of the Second Division. "I was a footballing centre half, I didn't have the physicality or presence of Jim," he admits. "Off the field you couldn't meet a more gentle bloke but on it he was a monster. I remember coming up against Whymark of Ipswich and Osgood of Chelsea in my first few games for the club, formidable forwards. Jim went up before the games and basically threatened them, saying if they came near him he'd sort them out… and they never did! They always stayed out wide, out of the way of him. Once he took his teeth out and got on the pitch he was an animal. That wasn't me! Jim was a tremendous player, as was Martin. It was difficult. We went to places like York and Walsall and their centre forwards were huge and brutal. To go from the First Division where you could play football, to the Second Division where it was a lot more physical was a bit of a shock. I could look after myself, don't get me wrong, but even so…"

United were four points clear at the top of the League, and five points clear of Aston Villa who were in fourth, just outside of the promotion places, yet the manager also felt that the team was in need of some refreshment and reinvigoration. Though the timing of the transfer which brought Steve Coppell to Old Trafford couldn't have been better (and may have been hastened in light of recent form), the Tranmere Rovers wide man had in fact been scouted by the club for quite some time. Johnny Carey, Norman Scholes and the great Jimmy Murphy had all watched the 19 year-old and on Thursday, February 27th, Manchester United completed a modest £40,000 transfer with a further £20,000 to follow after Coppell had made twenty league appearances. "Our check on him has been very thorough," said Docherty. "I think he's a very good player and now it's up to him to take his big opportunity." The Doc's intuition was shared by Liverpool manager Bill Shankly, who had said to Docherty in a telephone conversation that he shared a lot of characteristics with Kevin Keegan.

United were easily able to afford the fee - the initial transfer fee was identical to the one they had just received from Southampton for McCalliog, who had spent less than a year at Old Trafford but had made his mark. Signed to provide the goals the club were desperately lacking in the relegation run in of the previous season, he'd notched 4 in 11 league games. He had featured regularly in the Second Division but wasn't an automatic first choice and was voicing that opinion - with the pub incident, it may well have been the point where Docherty had decided enough was enough. "It was the hardest thing of my life," said McCalliog, "But I wanted to enjoy my football." Like Ted MacDougall before him, McCalliog would return to haunt United and Docherty, featuring in the Saints team that triumphed over the Reds in the 1976 FA Cup Final.

The Coppell transfer caught most by surprise, including, it seems, the printers of the match programme for United's game against lowly Cardiff City on the first day of March.

MARCH

"KOPEL S" WAS LISTED in the match programme (the 'S' denoting substitute rather than his first name) - possibly down to an assumption that he was a relative of Frank Kopel, the Scottish defender who had played twelve times over a two season spell from 1967–69 (and, incidentally, famously scored an incredible goal for Dundee United against Anderlecht in 1979). Yet by 5pm that Saturday a star had been born, and nobody would be forgetting the name of Steve Coppell again.

SATURDAY 1ST MARCH - DIVISION TWO - OLD TRAFFORD (43,601)

MANCHESTER UNITED 4-0 CARDIFF CITY

Stepney, Forsyth, Houston[1], Greenhoff, James, Buchan, Morgan (Coppell), McIlroy[1], Pearson[1], Macari[1], Daly

Steve James was back in the starting line-up as his injury against Hull City wasn't as bad as first feared; Gerry Daly, too, was recalled after a spell out, with Mick Martin losing his place. "My main concern is to get us back on the winning trail after a rather erratic course lately," wrote Docherty in his programme notes. "I still feel there is no need for panic. As I pointed out here in the programme for our last home game, we need only average a point a game to make sure of promotion and if we can get a good result

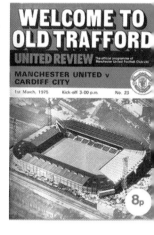

against Cardiff City this afternoon we shall be fully up to schedule. A lean spell was only to be expected, and the main thing is not to let it undermine our confidence. Of course the longer a poor time goes on the more worrying it becomes. We are certainly not taking it lightly at Old Trafford and there are a number of alternatives we have available to try and get the edge back in the team. So don't be too disheartened by the Villa result. They are a good team and to be beaten by them is no disgrace. What I am interested in now is our performance against Cardiff, a team we warmly welcome to Old Trafford."

The criticism of United may have been over the top but the concerns were quite genuine and thus it was a logical question to ask if the Reds were not quite as good as they had seemed. Going in to the game, with the knives sharpening in the press, it could be said that United were teetering on the edge of either being a temporarily profligate team lacking in confidence, or, simply, a team not very good at putting chances away.

With the logic that defeat can sometimes be good for a team, the nature of the setback at Aston Villa may have brought it home to one or two. Having just about recovered from the bitter blow of relegation, Docherty was now subscribing to the theory that defeat in certain situations was in fact crucial to progression and development. To be convincingly beaten by a better team on the day was a blow to the pride but would, hopefully, provoke a reaction.

Still, it took quite some time for United to get going against Cardiff, who went into the game in the bottom three. Cometh the hour, cometh the man, and a symbolic changing of the guard at Old Trafford. Steve Coppell was brought on for Willie Morgan (which, inevitably, caused ripples later on) but claims that the new man changed the game are a little disingenuous. Coppell was still trotting on to the pitch to try and assist United's attack from a corner (incidentally, to the sound of boos from supporters dissatisfied with Morgan leaving the game) when Greenhoff's corner was headed in by Stewart Houston, who opened the scoring at Old Trafford for the second game in a row.

Coppell was, however, hugely influential in the scoreline

Time was running out for Willie Morgan - subbed in the second half for Steve Coppell against Cardiff, the young Liverpudlian quickly established himself by setting up two goals. He would eventually usurp Morgan on the right wing.

becoming as impressive as it did. "After an hour of frustration, United sent on new boy Steve Coppell for Willie Morgan. His first touch sent the ball spinning into Stuart Pearson's path, who put the ball into the net for United's second goal," reported Bert Thorpe. "With four minutes left the 19-year-old former Tranmere lad crossed for Lou Macari to hit United's fourth goal. How's that for starters?"

The third goal was all about McIlroy. "The goal of the match, indeed the best at Old Trafford I have seen this season, came after a breathtaking 60 yard run by Sammy McIlroy," wrote Thorpe. "The Irishman picked up a clearance inside his own half and raced away hotly pursued by half a dozen Cardiff men. They never gained an inch on him and Irwin was beaten as he vainly left his goal." United had been in thrilling form in the last half hour though

Thorpe was hesitant in his praise. "Only then (after the second goal) did United move the ball about convincingly - but of course teams often do that when they're winning," he wrote.

McIlroy had been blossoming as the season progressed. "From the start of the season until the end of the blip, wherever he was able, the Doc was building a consistent side rather than the number of wholesale changes in the time before, and that was helping us to knit together, build partnerships and discover our best form," he recalls. "We were confident of turning it around but the signing of Steve Coppell gave us a great boost at just the right time. People had never heard of him and thought he wouldn't cope but he settled in right away."

Coppell, too, was delighted afterwards. "It was fantastic playing here. The boss told me to play wide on the right and enjoy myself and that's just what I did," said the Liverpudlian, after sharing that he had had to borrow a pair of boots from Stuart Pearson. Docherty, too, was understandably pleased, describing Coppell as a 'great prospect' but was less enamoured with Morgan, who had gone straight home after being brought off, though appeared to show empathy. "It's never nice for a player to be substituted," said Docherty, continuing, "they don't like it, but Willie Morgan must realise this is a 12-man game. Anyway, I was right, the result proved it... if he played well enough, he would keep Coppell out - and vice versa. That's the way it has to be."

With more than a couple of hundred appearances for the club and a hugely popular personality that supporters adored, it was never going to be a pleasant scenario to see Willie Morgan marginalised on the sidelines. Morgan was such an important player and this was such an important recurring story throughout the season that it simply could not be excluded from this record. Morgan had clearly grown unhappy with how he felt the manager was treating him, but on the other hand, by and large Docherty could at least point to the direct results of his team selections as justification for the tough calls he'd had to make. More than any other time, and mainly because of the arrival and form of Coppell, Morgan's future at the club was now in severe doubt.

It didn't go down well. A United supporter, Elizabeth Wynne, created a petition to demand that Morgan was recalled to the starting line up and request a public reason to explain why he wasn't in it. To his credit, Docherty responded to simply say that the result had justified his decision and he didn't want to change a winning team. He also took the first available opportunity to put across his version of events in his own words, in the programme notes for the next home game against Norwich later in the month. "The signing of young Steve Coppell has given us cover for Willie Morgan at outside right. Incidentally a lot of people seem to be making more of the that issue than necessary," insisted the Doc. "Willie is one of our more senior players and I just would not be doing my job if I did not have someone ready to carry on the tremendous work Willie has done for the club over the years."

Evidently, with Morgan's time at the club about to end, people in fact weren't making more out of the issue, but Docherty's claims otherwise can be put down to a manager wanting a steady ship with the run-in in mind, rather than dishonesty. Morgan may well have felt that he was forced out because that is the natural human reaction to seeing someone come in like Coppell did. Could Morgan have stayed on and been a squad member? He was too good for that and he had contributed so much that he didn't deserve to go out like that. Morgan would move on and enjoy success elsewhere, United would move on too. To his credit, Morgan had never criticised Coppell and nobody could argue that he wasn't a worthy successor.

It was a time of change at United but one that Docherty felt was necessary at a critical moment in the season when confidence was wavering. Heading into the local derby with Bolton Wanderers, the new found optimism generated by the Cardiff result (despite the Morgan fallout) and the signing of Coppell was hopefully going to manifest itself in another good result.

SATURDAY 8TH MARCH - DIVISION TWO - BURNDEN PARK (37,759)

BOLTON WANDERERS 0-1 MANCHESTER UNITED

Stepney, Forsyth, Houston (Young), Greenhoff, James, Buchan, Coppell, McIlroy, Pearson[1], Macari, Daly

It's fair to say that in his second outing for United, Coppell enjoyed a fairly mixed afternoon. He started in the number seven shirt for the first time and acquitted himself fairly well against former Reds star, Tony Dunne - well enough to receive praise from the manager afterwards, with Docherty proclaiming, "He's got the chance to become a great player once he gets fitter." Those positives were contrasted by the failure to take a golden opportunity to score, and also by receiving a

booking. The yellow card was for not retreating ten yards in a wall from a free kick - which, for Coppell, would have been a source of great irritation considering he had publicly said he wanted to go throughout his career without picking up a caution.

He did at least play his part in the only goal of the game. "From a corner by Coppell on the right, Stuart (sic) Houston headed against the bar," reported Les Taylor. "The Bolton defence stood watching and Pearson headed inside the left-hand post and the ball rebounded to him." It seemed the host defence were caught cold by Pearson's predatory instinct, which is a surprise given that their match programme noted "He has had to spend several weeks on the sidelines through injuries; even so, he is still top scorer."

Bolton were managed by former United defender Ian Greaves who stated he had "a great regard for the club (United) and their traditions, but all that counts for nothing as Bolton Wanderers go out for the points." Despite those words – and Bolton's own need for points in the promotion race – United's defence was rarely troubled, aside from one moment early in the second half, when Houston was forced to take a break from attacking duties and perform his more conventional defensive role, heading off the line from a corner. It came at a price – he fell awkwardly, aggravating an injury he'd picked up earlier in the match, and being forced to come off. "It was worth it," he proudly said later.

It was yet another all-ticket game but once more hooliganism grabbed headlines; "50 Fans Hurt In Terracing Clash" read one report that continued with the news that 70 fans had been ejected, fifty had treatment for injuries, and 32 fans were due to appear in court (from 34 arrested). The *Daily Telegraph* reported that one of the injured was a policeman, who had been struck by a flying brick. "Yesterday police praised licensees who closed before the match or employed doormen," reported the *Telegraph*. "The licensees were yesterday counting the cost of their decision to close. One near the football ground estimated that it had cost him at least £100."

Pearson's goal was the decider but it was Macari once more who was the star man. "He was definitely the best player on the pitch and should be in the Scotland team to play Sweden in April," enthused Docherty. Macari had carried the mantle of top scorer in Pearson's absence and even though the former Hull man had surpassed him in all competitions, Macari could at least be proud of being the top scorer in the League Cup that season – the first United player to do so.

Victory had moved United back to a five point advantage over Sunderland – six over Aston Villa in third, and seven over Norwich

City, the club's next opponents. Norwich, of course, had proven themselves to be a real thorn in United's side (although they had ultimately fallen to defeat in the League Cup Final), but Docherty was full of confidence regardless going into the game.

"People have been trying to say that the bubble has burst at Old Trafford. Don't believe it!" he wrote in his programme notes. "We kick off against Norwich City at Old Trafford this afternoon still five points clear at the top of the Second Division, so I don't think our bad spell could have been quite so serious as some critics have been trying to make out. I knew it would come right in the end. It was just a matter of keeping confident and sticking at it... Everything fitted into place (against Bolton), as I knew it would provided we kept playing football through our rocky spell which was a combination of injuries and loss of form. I try not to complain about injuries because they are something that happens to every team, but you certainly have to take them into account if you are trying to make out a case for a team losing its touch. I don't find it any coincidence that we have struck improved form since returning to full strength for selection, with the exception of course of Jim Holton."

SATURDAY 15TH MARCH - DIVISION TWO - OLD TRAFFORD (56,202)

MANCHESTER UNITED 1-1 NORWICH CITY

Stepney, Forsyth, Houston, Greenhoff, James, Buchan, Coppell (Young), McIlroy, Pearson[1], Macari, Daly

United were able to name an unchanged team, with Morgan again absent. In front of England manager Don Revie, Steve Coppell and Stuart Pearson combined early in the second half with the latter scoring from close range. It was his 16th goal of the season and his fourth since his latest return from injury.

The home side were enterprising enough but their visitors were game and had, of course, already achieved a result at Old Trafford that season – with a quarter of the game remaining, they grabbed an equaliser. The identity scorer of the goal barely needs an introduction – Ted MacDougall, who had gone past making a subtle note to now firmly rubber stamping the point, was captaining the Canaries for the day and led by example by netting.

Docherty made a change that was, on the face of it, fairly defensive – Young for Coppell – but his team continued to push for both points with the better of the chances in the closing exchanges. Neither team was dissatisfied with a draw (particularly as Sunderland also drew on the day) and, in truth, neither side probably deserved anything more. United remained five points clear of their rivals with all head-to-heads against the main rivals for promotion negotiated.

Strangely for a match programme – and even more strange considering the identity of the manager – there were no 'manager's notes' in the Nottingham Forest publication for United's visit to the City Ground on March 22nd. Brian Clough had been in charge there for two and a half months after his well documented,

Steve James tackles debutant Martin Peters in another tightly contested tussle with The Canaries.

infamously disastrous spell at Elland Road and was apparently taking a sabbatical from speaking publicly after the equally infamous television interview with Don Revie. Clough had claimed he was sacked for poor results after just six games at Leeds but his start at Forest hadn't gone much better; they had won his first game, a Cup replay against Tottenham Hotspur, and their next, a League game against Fulham, but hadn't won in twelve games since.

There was, however, still a very strongly worded section of the match programme, in the form of a curious advertisement from local sportswear stockists Redmayne & Todd. "Warning from Redmaynes," a big bold red heading declared. "adidas the world famous '3-striped' soccer shoes should only be worn by the best players on the field, and not by 'Forest' supporters," read the advert. "However, adidas suggest that if you must wear the famous '3-striped' sports equipment, that you contact Redmayne

& Todd Ltd., Carrington Street, Nottingham (official suppliers to Nottingham Forest F.C.) who stock the full range of adidas sports and recreation clothing and equipment."

SATURDAY 22ND MARCH - DIVISION TWO - CITY GROUND (21,893)

NOTTINGHAM FOREST 0-1 MANCHESTER UNITED

Stepney, Forsyth, Houston, Greenhoff, James, Buchan, Coppell, McIlroy, Pearson, Macari, Daly[1]

Clough may have bitten his tongue before the game but was keen to talk after seeing his side go down to a 36th minute goal from Gerry Daly. "Brian Clough was envious. Not because Manchester United carried away two points that might have removed some of the fear from Forest's future, but because they did it with a panache he sees little hope of producing in his own side," reported Peter Johnson. "Believe it or not – and I for one, couldn't – this was our best

performance since I took over," said Clough. "Against any other side we might have won. But we were up against a class side... a class Second Division side, that is. I've seen all the top teams in the division, including Sunderland and Villa, and I'd say that United play thirty percent more football than any of their main rivals. Good luck to them in the First Division, because they've done it with skill."

Despite his reputation for being outspoken, Clough could also be the most sportsmanlike and gracious manager to a rival – a kindred spirit for Docherty, then, some might say (though the Doc confesses to still learning this at this point!). Strangely, Docherty was relatively reserved afterwards, sending a reminder to his team that he still felt they required four more points from their remaining seven matches in order to secure promotion. They had taken seven from their last eight, with Villa, Sunderland and Norwich now tied on 42 points (seven behind United), though Villa and Norwich had a game in hand. Mathematically, United required seven points to be certain of promotion, which tied in with the managers previous theory of a point a game being enough, though in his mind, recent victories had brought the target much closer.

Whatever the reasoning, United had crossed the bridge from favourites and runaway leaders to virtually guaranteed Champions in recent weeks, with it now being a matter of if and not when it would be confirmed. The win at Forest had made a great difference in this, and despite his low-key response, Docherty'a only disappointment from the day would have been that he never felt secure enough of the result to give Jimmy Nicholl a run out.

The games were coming thick and fast in March and with the Easter weekend on the horizon, United were faced with playing three games in four days. The perceived 'packed' holiday schedules of the contemporary game had nothing on this! Fortunately for United, as Docherty had earlier remarked, there was a relatively clean bill of health in his squad, and he was able to take the rare chance to name an unchanged side for the fourth consecutive game.

With everyone in the same position of having to play these games, United were not at a disadvantage, and in fact, with the respectively low positions of their opponents over Easter, they were approaching them in the knowledge that a good Bank Holiday could see them on the brink of the target they'd been fighting for all season.

GOOD FRIDAY, 28TH MARCH - DIVISION TWO - EASTVILLE STADIUM (19,337)

BRISTOL ROVERS 1-1 MANCHESTER UNITED

Stepney, Forsyth, Houston, Greenhoff, James (Morgan), Buchan, Coppell, McIlroy, Pearson, Macari[1], Daly

As Lou Macari mentioned earlier, part of the charm of United's season in Division Two was the opportunity for supporters to travel to different places. Bristol Rovers' Eastville Stadium (also known as the Bristol Stadium) was certainly different, being also a host for greyhound racing (and, in 1977, motorcycle speedway racing). The arena had been constructed near a gas holder, which led to the nickname of 'the Gasheads' that the supporters adopted – finally, to round off the quirky character of Eastville, there were flower beds behind each goal.

It was a stadium, however, that United fans were fairly familiar with – their most recent encounter being a 1972 League Cup tie, with FA Cup games there in 1956 and 1964. However, this was the Reds' first ever League game there. Rovers manager Don Megson was hopeful that his side, marginally above the relegation places, could benefit from the 'leveller' that he described as the end of season 'jitters'. "United will be under as much pressure as we are," he insisted, "and I'm sure our fans will give the right kind of vocal support... Manchester is my home town so that is an extra incentive – although I don't think one is needed – for us to win today."

Macari's own recent form hadn't quite been rewarded with the goals it probably deserved but he managed to atone for that here with an absolute blockbuster of a strike from a cross by Houston. The goal settled the Reds who had been forced into a tactical reshuffle following an injury to Steve James - an aggravation of the ankle knock he'd been carrying since the Hull game – which forced the defender to come off. Willie Morgan was back in the squad for the first time in four weeks and came on, with Greenhoff moving back into the centre of defence. United were firmly in control and created a number of chances, though were unable to convert any. Late on, a Bristol Rovers attack encouraged Stepney out of his goal to try and make the target smaller – instead, David Staniforth found Bruce Bannister (whose place in the side was announced so late he wasn't even named in the squad on the match-day programme) and as time stood still for the visiting supporters, he finished with aplomb into the empty goal to give his team an unexpected point. "No dramatist in the world could have written a part like that. It was live theatre at its best," declared an excited Bannister afterwards, with his exhilaration the undoubted reason for his hyperbole.

The goal and result helped Bristol Rovers in their quest to avoid relegation – they finished in the final safe position of 19th. Docherty had set his team a target of at least four points from the Easter programme and was disappointed to have not gotten halfway there. "I'm disappointed at having victory snatched from us right at the end and I feel sorry for the lads because of the way they worked. It was really ironic because Alex Stepney had nothing to do. At one stage he appeared so frozen standing on his line that I was thinking of going round and giving him my overcoat!" quipped the manager.

The game had been preceded by an interesting story where the hosts had planned to implement a 15 pence 'hooligan tax' on United's support. With the potential money raised, Rovers had approached Viewsport, a closed circuit television company, to broadcast the game. United's supporters were naturally very unhappy and neither were the club, as the proposal would have meant an 11am kick off. The Football League rejected the application.

United's Saturday game was against York City, and with the rapid turnaround of games, Docherty's programme notes had been written before the game against Bristol Rovers - but they carried a fairly prophetic warning. "We seem to have made a habit of giving away gift goals against Norwich this season, I don't say it is bad luck either, more like bad professionalism," he lamented. "Frequently I have been more worried about our mistakes than anything the opposition might do. I know we have a good defence – the goals against figures prove that – but if we could wipe out the unforced slips it would be even better."

Still, Docherty was in positive mood in what he described 'could be the crucial weekend for Manchester United'. "I must say that I am very happy about our recovery of form," he expressed. "A few weeks ago our results were far from championship figures. Three points from five games was poor, but note the improvement from the next five games with a return of seven points. That was certainly championship form and a neat little run after a bad spell that put us back on the right track."

York City – themselves battling relegation – had also changed managers during the season, with a familiar name, Wilf McGuinness, taking charge. It was McGuinness of course who had taken what to some might have seemed like the poisoned chalice, being the first man to attempt to succeed Sir Matt Busby at Manchester United. Luck had not been his friend and ultimately he was dismissed; after four years in Greece, coaching Aris Thessaloniki and Panachaiki, in February 1975 he had been given the York job. It was his first return to Old Trafford.

SATURDAY 29TH MARCH - DIVISION TWO - OLD TRAFFORD (46,802)

MANCHESTER UNITED 2-1 YORK CITY

Stepney, Forsyth, Houston, Morgan[1], Greenhoff, Buchan, Coppell, McIlroy, Pearson, Macari[1], Daly

"Wilf was more nervous than the players," claimed visiting defender Barry Swallow, despite this being the largest League crowd York had ever played in front of. The only notable action of the first half was an injury to the linesman in the 28th minute - play was stopped while the search for a replacement went on, and eventually, it took an announcement from the public address system to source somebody from the crowd to do it!

The confidence of recent form wasn't helping United's cause (though it may have only been natural that their resources were drained) and it took until the 75th minute for the breakthrough to finally come. Forsyth's free kick was flicked on by Houston, and Morgan (in the number four shirt, not his usual number seven) was on hand to finish from close in. Ten minutes later, Macari found space in the penalty area after a pass from Morgan (who originally appeared to control the ball with his hand), but was brought down. He gesticulated for a penalty but referee Pat Partridge waved it away - still in control of the ball, Macari promptly jumped up and smashed it into the goal.

The points were safe but Docherty was left to curse another late lack of concentration when York went straight down the field and scored through Jimmy Seal. Of the two managers, though, McGuinness was the one angrier at full time. "Two bad decisions cost us the game. I didn't think it should have been a free kick that led to the first goal and Morgan clearly handled before the second was scored," he argued.

McGuinness recalled the return in his 2008 autobiography. "It felt overwhelmingly peculiar to be operating from the away dugout, but there was absolutely no question of divided loyalties," he said. "I was very proud of how my team played. I think we deserved a point and the goal by Lou Macari which turned out to be the difference between the sides was an outrage. The little fella caught the ball in both hands, ran with it for ten yards and then drop-kicked it into our net – at least, that's how I remember it!"

Jokes aside, McGuinness was left touched by the welcome he received by both the club and the United manager. "I was profoundly moved, too, by the warmth of the reception I received at Old Trafford. The fans were fantastic, greeting me with genuine affection and appreciation, together with a dash of sympathy over the way I'd had to leave... Then there was Tommy Docherty, the current boss, who could not have made me more welcome. The Doc can be a contradictory customer because he says some outrageous things at times, but he can also be one of the most supportive men in football. When I had broken my leg all those years earlier, one of the first letters I received was from Tommy, outlining how he had made a complete recovery after breaking his own leg and predicting that I would do the same. It was a lovely touch because he was an established star at the time and I hardly knew him. You never forget generosity of spirit like that."

Showing the kind of spirit they had at Old Trafford, McGuinness' York City stayed up. In his future career as an after dinner speaker, one of his many soundbites was that he had 'managed York City in the Fourth, Third and Second Divisions – just in the wrong order!' after two consecutive relegations in 1976 and 1977.

Manchester United's game with York City may not seem remarkable but it was the game which saw the birth of Docherty's 4-2-4 formation which would sweep all before it the following season. The 4-4-2 that had been the shape for most of the season was slowly being advanced, possibly through the attacking capabilities of his side and the way that they had naturally fallen together. As was stated earlier, Brian Greenhoff's permanent move into the back four was made the following season, but that is where he played against York City. Morgan and Coppell were both wide men but Docherty's interpretation of the capabilities of each player were perhaps best illustrated in his subtle, yet profound description of the two - Morgan being an outside right, and Coppell being a winger. The irony, of course, is that of the two, Coppell was undoubtedly the grafter in comparison, with Morgan probably a more natural 'winger' with his penchant for the incredible. Daly and Macari as midfielders could not exactly be said to be defensive minded, but equally, were not work shy. McIlroy was up front with Pearson. Eventually, McIlroy would move further back in place of Daly, and Jimmy Greenhoff and Gordon Hill would come in to complete the shape of the side.

Docherty openly confesses that the permanent Brian Greenhoff switch was almost 'an accident' although maybe he does not give himself due credit; Greenhoff had been used at centre half often enough for the manager to be aware of the defensive, and attacking, qualities he brought to the team in whichever role he played. Likewise, if pressed, he may well concede that the injury to Steve James against Bristol Rovers was the reason for the seed of this tactical revolution being planted rather than planned.

One of the many anecdotes told of Docherty and by the man himself is that he would heavily concentrate on emphasising his own team's quality in home games. That Tommy Cavanagh would frequently walk into the dressing room with opposition team-sheets and screw them up, with the message that the opponents were inconsequential. It is plain to see, however, that a great deal of consideration went into the preparation of this team. It was not just a series of convenient accidents. In later years some players to come through the youth system at the club would refer to Cavanagh as unnecessarily harsh but this was in keeping with a tough breeding ground for players which included facilities which received mixed reviews from those who lived through the time. Some felt that The Cliff was just as good as anywhere else, others – like Brian Greenhoff, for example – would go on record as saying that United were not even as well equipped for training as Burnley.

It would be unnecessarily sycophantic to declare that Docherty was the creator of football tactics in the modern era but just as he doesn't give himself the credit for the subtle changes which made such a difference, it should commonly be accepted that he isn't given the credit by a majority who seem to think Manchester United Football Club went from Sir Matt Busby to Sir Alex Ferguson and the years in between were all a terrible dream. Ferguson was pretty open about following Busby's blueprint, particularly in the sense that the club ought to have a successful youth system. That much is faithful to the philosophy which Busby and Jimmy Murphy put in place.

Though the use of orthodox wingers was hardly alien to Manchester United (indeed, Busby was fond of playing them), it had been a long time since conventional right sided and left sided wide men were implemented. That, of course, was mostly down to the brilliant George Best causing havoc all over the front line. In selecting a 4-2-4, Docherty was proceeding with a structure that would go on to not only be the hallmark of his side but also, arguably, that of the successful Manchester United side of the 1990's and beyond under Sir Alex Ferguson. It could even be contended that until Louis van Gaal's implementation of a three man defence in July 2014, and evolution of the midfield shape throughout the season, Docherty's Manchester United shape had been in place for forty years.

"I think that might be fair," agrees McIlroy. "The tradition of great wingers at the club preceded Tommy Docherty with Willie Morgan and John Aston under Sir Matt but they were usually joined by George Best – and he wasn't a winger in the traditional sense. Jonny and Willie were out and out wingers. But when Stevie and Willie played on the wings, they were two proper wingers... and since then we've always been renowned for having great wingers. Sir Matt loved wingers, and when the Doc put in the 4-2-4 system, it was just great to see. It was great to play in, too, for the likes of me, Gerry and Lou. Alls we loved doing was getting the ball, doing our little bit and then giving it the wingers. We used to play some unbelievable one touch, off the cuff football. It was unbelievable to play in."

Ferguson's most successful and entertaining teams were (arguably) his 1994 and 1999 sides, which both used what was ostensibly a 4-4-2. Or was it? Ryan Giggs was a left winger who had played up front and through the middle as a youngster – Andrei Kanchelskis was a right sided winger whose only thought was to attack and score. The 1994 side was as much a 4-2-4 as the 1977 team was. Kanchelskis was replaced by David Beckham (a re-imagining of a Morgan to Coppell transition) for the 1999 team. The midfield engine room was made up of box to box players, though admittedly, the 94 and 99 sides were more defensively minded. No, Docherty didn't create the 4-4-2 or 4-2-4 but his use of the systems at Manchester United were very much his own and surely it is too much of a coincidence to feel that Ferguson, with his vast experience and knowledge, was unaware of the systems implemented by the Doc, considering the familiarities between that and his teams. Still, Docherty didn't even warrant a single mention in Ferguson's 1999 autobiography 'Managing My Life'.

Without a doubt, this is another of those points where we jump forward in time and consider hypotheticals and what if's. As logical or illogical the suggestion that the development of this embryonic 4-2-4 and the roles of the players within in it played a major part in the modern day successes of Manchester United, it is of course sure without a shadow of a conceivable doubt that the 2-1 victory over York City were the first signs we saw of what would be the 'classic' Docherty side.

Two home games in three days meant two match programmes and, consequently, two manager's columns. Tommy Docherty was never short for something to say but even so, discussing the various events, implications and permutations that normally went into his notes was going to be a stretch when there were two games that would pass before this publication was released. Docherty's notes were introduced with a general reference to it being a 'crunch' time in the football calendar, but continued with a look into the future - with personnel, rather than tactics, the focus.

"All eyes are focused on the first team at the moment. It is the crunch weekend, as I wrote in Saturday's programme, and I am looking for a big effort against Oldham Athletic this afternoon," said Docherty. "But Easter is not just important for the Second Division championship, it is also a vital point in preparation for the future. The Easter school holidays are the time when we take on apprentice professional players from school and at the same time we have been busy making decisions about the apprentices who have been at Old Trafford for the last 12 months. The other day we took Peter Loughnane on to our full-time professional staff after completing his apprenticeship. His parents came up for his 17th birthday from Shrewsbury where he played as a schoolboy. They saw the "digs" where he lives in Manchester and looked over our training set-up at the Cliff. They met Frank Blunstone, our youth coach, Norman Scholes, our chief scout who did the original work bringing the boy to Old Trafford, and all the other staff involved in trying to make our facilities for young people the best in the game."

To some, the extensive notes may have been seen as garrulous, but do at least reflect Docherty's determination to bring through young players. Across from the notes was a bulletin from the Club desk – "Manchester United are seeking accommodation for young players, ideally within a four mile radius of either Old Trafford or The Cliff Ground, Broughton. Anyone who feels they may have suitable accommodation should write or telephone, Mr. N Scholes, Chief Scout, 061-872-1661."

In his "Club Topics" programme column for the forthcoming Fulham game, David Meek heralded the work done at the club beyond the first team. "The Reds are bounding back with a very young side and an even younger reserve team," he said. "The average age of the League team is 22 and last weekend the reserves had eight 17-year-old players in their side. United are putting great emphasis on youth in their rebuilding and quality rather than quantity is the keyword in the recruitment of schoolboys these days. The club have just made two more important schoolboy signings, taking Martyn Rogers from the Nottingham area and Kevan Poppett from County Durham as associated schoolboys. Rogers is a 15-year-old full back who has also played for the England Under-15 team and elected to come to Old Trafford despite fierce competition from other professional clubs. Poppett, a 16-year-old defender, is captain of the Durham Under-19 team and has already had two games for the 'B' team with United... From time to time there has been criticism of what the big League clubs do for youngsters they take from all over the country as raw school kids. But United can proudly say that of the nearly 100 apprentices they have signed since the scheme started in 1960, only 18 failed to make the grade, some of them leaving for reasons other than football. Years ago many clubs left them too much to their own devices, but now they train every morning and practise special skills in the afternoons. 'We have two full-time professional coaches to look after about a dozen boys; it is a better staffing ratio than Manchester Grammar School', says chief scout Norman Scholes. A great deal of care is taken matching a boy's background for the right digs. Parents are taken to meet the landladies and reports are sent home. Schooling is encouraged and last summer United flew four boys home from a youth tournament in Switzerland to sit 'O' and 'A' level examinations. Alan Kirkup, Jimmy Kelly, Lindsay McKeown and Kenny Fitzpatrick had all been studying and rather than allow them to miss the exams they were brought back to Manchester and then flown back to the football tournament again. Former headmaster Scholes says: "The set-up for boys is now better than ever before. This I can honestly say to parents and Tommy Docherty is so co-operative that whatever I ask just happens." United are now so determined to make sure that their youngsters do not waste their time that next season the traditional job of apprentices cleaning football boots will be scrapped. 'Our apprentices are precious material, too valuable for us to use as cheap labour. They are no longer going to be employed on any menial tasks like sweeping out the stands. The idea that brewing tea and running errands in a boy's formative years is character building is a myth,' he added."

Away from the long term plans for a successful Manchester United, the short term ambitions were to achieve promotion as soon as possible. Results elsewhere meant a win in the Easter Monday game with Oldham Athletic couldn't secure promotion, but it could give them one foot firmly planted back into the First Division.

MONDAY 31ST MARCH - DIVISION TWO
OLD TRAFFORD (56,618)

MANCHESTER UNITED 3-2 OLDHAM ATH.

Stepney, Forsyth, Houston, Morgan, Greenhoff, Buchan, Coppell[1], McIlroy[1], Pearson, Macari[1], Daly (Martin)

With all the talk being of the exciting future that hopefully lay in store, it was probably inevitable given the sometimes seemingly contrived nature of football scripts that the past would have its say. Oldham Athletic put on a spirited show that defied their precarious place on the edge of the relegation zone but Willie Morgan inspired United to a thrilling victory. It was undoubtedly the unexpected open performance of the Latics which contributed to a game described by journalist Ian Gibb as

United's 'finest showing at home for many weeks'. Gibb lavished praise on Morgan's performance, saying that it should have helped United to be well in front at the break. "They had to settle for McIlroy's 22nd minute goal when he snapped up Morgan's centre," he wrote. "United were rocked back on their heels in the third minute of the second half when a hard cross from McVitie was touched back by Young, for Robins to drill in the equaliser. United, however, would not be denied and four minutes later, Macari added the final touch to a Morgan corner, via the head of McIlroy. Macari admitted afterwards he put the ball in with his elbow. He told me: 'When the ball came over from McIlroy's back header the goalkeeper was shaping to save it. I knocked it in with my elbow.' Then came Coppell's hammer blow, only for Young to head Oldham back into the game with 15 minutes left. But United's third biggest crowd of the season – 56,618 – were determined to cheer their team to the title."

Another report said 'United might have had a cricket score in the first 45 minutes as they launched attack after attack' in what was described as a 'leagues apart' first half. Coppell's well hit right foot effort from an angle was his first goal for the club and a crucial one, following another controversial Macari moment so soon after the last.

With victory, United had reached 54 points – surpassing the 53 point target Docherty had set which he had estimated would guarantee promotion. The manager himself said afterwards that they'd done enough. "That's promotion now," he declared. "It's been hard, but our target was to get back at the first attempt."

However, the Reds, though almost there, were left waiting for another day to finally celebrate.

Alex Stepney punches clear during the derby with Oldham Athletic

APRIL

THE RETURN TO THE TOP FLIGHT may have taken a little longer than expected but once it had become an inevitability in early March, United's form had improved not only in results but in performances. The assurance had returned and the swagger returned, though this may well have had something to do with the approach of other clubs, whose own need for points meant they were forced to at least try and take the game to United. At least, that's the ostensible reason - one might expect that teams like York and Oldham would have taken the 'Portsmouth' approach, but even though United supporters had to wait until the latter stages for the Easter home wins, there was no suggestion that that was down to unyielding back lines.

Well, the wait for the ultimate prize of promotion was almost over, although it too had gone into the 'latter stages', so to speak. The Division had proven to be far more competitive than it had been for Middlesbrough the previous season and, of course, United were always the target that caused teams to raise their game.

For Southampton - a club firmly lodged in mid-table - the opportunity to play Manchester United was one they wanted to savour. "The visit of Manchester United has, over the years, always produced crowds well in excess of the average, and whilst at the time of writing ticket sales have not gone as well as expected, I feel sure that an increased attendance today will help bring about an atmosphere to which the players will react and ensure that the very best skills come from the many talented players out on the park today," wrote Saints manager Lawrie McMenemy in his programmes notes.

Elsewhere in the programme, the hosts were joining in with the premature congratulations. "So Manchester United have achieved a quick return to the First Division and no one will argue that that is not their rightful place. For most of the post-war years, Manchester United stood for everything that is good about English football, they won the European Cup and worldwide respect," their 'Spotlight' section detailed. "They still have a very long way to go before they can recapture the glories they enjoyed during Sir Matt Busby's managerial reign, but Tommy Docherty has had to plan in stages. That he has achieved his first objective – promotion – is something of which he can feel justifiable pride. Let's be honest. No other Second Division club has been able to hold a candle to the Reds this season. Though they showed signs of faltering in the New Year, their huge lead cushioned them against any serious disaster. Now they have regained their old killer instinct."

SATURDAY 5TH APRIL - DIVISION TWO - THE DELL (21,866)

SOUTHAMPTON 0-1 MANCHESTER UNITED

Stepney, Forsyth, Houston, Young, Greenhoff, Buchan (Martin), Morgan, McIlroy, Pearson, Macari[1], Daly

Lining up against the Reds was familiar face Jim McCalliog. The Scot would not have the same kind of impact as Norwich's MacDougall but Docherty was still left annoyed after the game with a former player. Not McCalliog, rather, Peter Osgood, who Docherty had coached through his formative years at Chelsea. Osgood was in aggressive mood, first of all being booked for a first half challenge on Morgan (who was in his number seven shirt as Coppell was rested),

then somehow escaping red for a reckless challenge on Macari.

"He could have broken his leg," fumed Docherty afterwards, referring to Osgood's challenge on Macari. "Ossie crawled into a hole (after the goal). You should have seen his head drop. Who wants players like that? Anybody who tried to do what he did to Macari is a cheat." Interestingly, Osgood had been a name linked with United during the 1973/74 season.

In front of a crowd that was still the biggest at the Dell that season (the biggest had been for the visit of Bristol City the previous week at 21,019), the game was brought into life after a fractured first half by the award of a 54th minute penalty to the hosts, right in front of the travelling supporters. Southampton legend Mick Channon stepped up to take it and sent Stepney the wrong way - fortunately for United, although Stepney had been the man who conceded the penalty, he didn't concede from the spot, as Channon hit the outside of the post and the ball bounced to safety.

Given a reprieve, United were still persevering for a winner and it was fitting in the context of the game and the season that it was Lou Macari who grabbed it - Macari was motivated by the earlier injustice but had put in performances of this nature all season. Sammy McIlroy intercepted a pass and cleverly found Macari; the diminutive Scot raced with the ball and finished from just inside he box. "I was so angry that after that tackle it was a case of me getting sent off or scoring a goal. I was desperate to score," admitted Macari.

After missing the opportunity to field Jimmy Nicholl at Forest, Docherty gave the young defender his Manchester United debut here, bringing him on in the 85th minute for Martin Buchan who had suffered a knock. Nicholl became Osgood's latest victim, receiving an elbow to the face as soon as he came on.

Perhaps it was the long journey (both metaphoric and literal), or maybe even the unnecessarily rough match they'd endured, but United's reaction to being promoted as a result of Macari's goal was a little understated. Buchan summarised the mood best.

*At last! Lou Macari acrobatically drives home the winner that seals
United's return to the First Division at the first attempt*

"Somehow I felt we should have all been running up and down, shouting and singing," he admitted to journalist Peter Johnson. "It seems to have been coming for so long now that we all seemed to accept it as inevitable. There were no wild celebrations, just the usual after-the-match routine."

It is interesting to observe the contrast the modern day recollections of the players – particularly Buchan and Macari, whose memories seem to almost defy their attitudes at the time. Macari was all effort, giving everything for the cause every week and growing in importance and stature as he did so. Buchan, as he noted, had sensed there was an inevitability for quite some time. Today, Macari says that the players found it easy over time, while Buchan protests the opposite. The captain explains more about that good natured disagreement with a fondness not normally associated with someone typecast as such an individual. "I was number six and he was normally ten so we didn't change together on match days but Lou and I stripped next to each other at the Cliff for years. He used to love winding me up and it was good fun," says Buchan. "He was the court jester, ably supported by Ashley Grimes, they were great times. Lou just loved making mischief. He says that we won the Second Division at a canter... I always say to him that it was very different for him. If we hit a ball for him and he thought it was too long, then he didn't have to chase it. If they sent a ball over my head, I can't say I'll leave it. You can't relax at the back. You can never take your foot off the gas. I will never say Lou didn't work hard though. He had a wonderful engine, was a ninety minute man and that's for sure. He wouldn't stay down from a knock even if he was hurt. We earned the right to win the league the way we did and when we had to battle we did that too."

There was still something to battle for - the glory of finishing as Champions - and the security of a seven point gap with 3 games to play (although Aston Villa were ten points behind with 3 games in hand) meant that should United keep winning, the Championship would be won before the final day.

With that in mind, mid-table Fulham were probably the ideal visitors to Old Trafford, with a promotion place only really achievable by the combination of six teams suffering collapses above them. Additionally, they had qualified for the FA Cup Final, meaning the extra probability of players being conscious about going in too heavily on challenges.

Following the game at the Dell, Docherty had been as understated as the occasion, saying, "I've got a team capable of surviving in the First Division."

By the time that the Fulham game came around, he was in far more optimistic spirits. "Manchester United are back in the First Division," he opened his programme notes, continuing, "It gives me tremendous satisfaction to be able to say that because I felt relegation very keenly. My lifelong ambition had been to become manager at Old Trafford and to achieve it by being the man who took them into the Second Division was a very bitter experience. But now I have put the record straight and clinched promotion, with a bit to spare, at the first attempt. Perhaps this weekend will also see us win the championship as well. My view is that 56 points will be enough to take the title, though that won't stop us trying to celebrate in style against Fulham this afternoon. I was delighted with our win at Southampton because it gave us promotion without dashing to hear the results from other grounds; but then I think we can claim to have set that kind of pace all season. We got away to a good start and have not really looked back since. The opening was important because it showed that the players had adopted the right attitude. I remember writing in the very first programme of the season that we must aim to match the spirit and aggression of our opponents. I said that if we could ally the right attitude to our skill then we would be all right.

"And that is how I think it has worked out. It is the factor that I think has been the key to our successful campaign. Also important has been the strength of our reserves. Jim Holton's broken leg and Stuart Pearson's struggle with a hamstring injury were major set-backs, yet we proved to have players capable of taking their place. Steve James and Arnie Sidebottom were tremendous and more recently Brian Greenhoff has stepped in. In fact I look at big Jim and Steve James and wonder how they are going to get back into the side! The whole staff have played their part and by that I mean on the training side and our whole set-up as well as the players. I think we can safely claim to deserve our promotion, simply because we have proved to be the best team in the Second Division. We achieved consistency in our winning results, and at the same time we have played attacking, entertaining football. We shall try to continue this in the First Division next season. I can't say I have been grateful for our year in the Second Division. I would have much preferred to have plodded along somewhere in mid-table while I went through the rebuilding process. As it was we had to continue the rebuilding in the Second Division and it is not always easy to get successful results during this kind of experiment and change. But we managed it, and we are going back with a team whose average age is only just over 22. That is a tremendous encouragement for the future. With such a young side there is obviously a lot of hard work ahead before we can really challenge for the top honours with conviction. I would ask for a couple of years to develop, and then I would say we will really be back in business. I said a year ago not to weep for Manchester United because out of the ashes of relegation will rise a team good enough to take on the world. Well we are not quite ready for that yet... but you have just seen the birth, the beginnings of what I sincerely believe will be another great era for Manchester United."

Docherty's words, as they often turned out to be this year, were once more prophetic, though even he may not have understood the profound effect the formation he selected for the visit of Fulham would have on the club's future, as he once more put the 4-2-4 that had been used against York into action, and this time, never looked back.

SATURDAY 12TH APRIL - DIVISION TWO - OLD TRAFFORD (52,971)

MANCHESTER UNITED 1-0 FULHAM

Stepney, Forsyth, Houston, Greenhoff, James, Morgan, Coppell, McIlroy, Pearson, Macari, Daly[1]

The supporters will not have been aware of the history they were watching but they were obviously hopeful of a landmark day – yet Aston Villa's win meant that mathematically, the club were still waiting for one more point despite putting Fulham away. It could, and should, have been another high scoring victory but United, as they had been too often, lacked a clinical edge and let Fulham off far too often.

Macari had rightly received much credit for his recent performances but man of the match today was Sammy McIlroy, whose direct, penetrative running always looked the most likely way that United would break through. It was inevitably through McIlroy that United gained their advantage in the match; one of his many dribbles was finished by a flashed cross that just evaded Pearson, but not Gerry Daly, who thumped the ball high into the net in the 21st minute.

From then on, the Reds played with freedom and creativity, getting the full backs involved at every opportunity. "...after giving Fulham a heavy first-half pounding their skill and hostility convinces me that they have nothing to fear in the top table," wrote journalist Ronald Crowther. "Willie Morgan, the winger recently out of favour, gave their attacking play a new dimension when operating down the left flank. Sammy McIlroy, who has played with ever-mounting confidence since Docherty gave him his chance to fulfill his boyhood promise was United's most persistent raider in a game in which better finishing by his teammates might have yielded more goals."

Fulham defender and English legend Bobby Moore was impressed by what he had seen. "They are certainly as good as any First Division side we have met this season," he said.

United's performance was convincing enough to leave supporters in celebratory mood. After the final whistle, more than 10,000 supporters remained in the Stretford End, singing 'Champions! Champions!' for over twenty minutes. Eventually, Tommy Docherty left the dressing room (where the champagne had already been cracked open) to acknowledge the loyal supporters.

The club had been due to play a testimonial for Pat Crerand at Old Trafford on Monday 14th April, with Liverpool the opponents. It was still being advertised in the programme for the Fulham game - Liverpool may well have been chosen as the team to face originally due to United not having a 'big' game as such in the run-in. In the Fulham programme, the inside cover included ticket information for the day, but on page 16, it was listed as a postponement with no reason given.

When the rescheduled game came around, it was United's current team taking on the 1968 European Cup winning side, a fitting event for somebody who had served the club so well.

Perhaps the cancellation was in anticipation of a hangover from Saturday's events (though, more likely, the fact that international football in the week would take away some players); as had become the theme, however, the anxiety of wanting to celebrate was delayed a little longer as United prepared for their final away game of the season.

"Manchester United were a loss to the First Division when relegated at the end of last season; and, such is their pulling power, they will be a loss to the Second," wrote their match programme. "It's their first Meadow Lane visit for exactly 40 years... and we have a hunch that it's probably going to be up to us, and the success of our efforts to reach the First Division, rather than United how long it will be before they come here again. So there could be no better way to bring down the Second Division curtain here until August than by saying 'Welcome, United!'"

SATURDAY 19TH APRIL - DIVISION TWO - MEADOW LANE (17,320)

NOTTS COUNTY 2-2 MANCHESTER UNITED

Stepney, Forsyth, Houston[1], Greenhoff,[1] James, Buchan, Coppell, McIlroy, Pearson, Macari, Daly

"Manchester United are back in the big-time as Second Division champs - but they nearly finished up as chumps by letting a two-goal lead slip away to put the vital point they needed in jeopardy," said one report. In a clichéd game of two halves, United raced into a commanding lead early on. Stewart Houston grabbed his 7th goal of the season from a Forsyth cross - the same combination, of course, which had brought about the club's first goal this campaign all the way back in

August at Leyton Orient. McIlroy brought his fine form from last week into this game and created the second goal with a cross for Brian Greenhoff to grab his first goal for eight months.

"Confident United thought they had sewn it up with a commanding lead at half time, but they were knocked off their pedestal by a second-half revival from Jimmy Sirrel's battlers," reported Tony Turner. "Eric Probert headed in a 49th minute goal to rock Tommy Docherty's defence and then transfer listed Kevin Randall - a regular source of danger - ghosted through unchallenged to snap up the equaliser."

United held on for a draw to earn the result that sealed the Second Division title - the final whistle prompted a pitch invasion, but the truth was that from minute one, the police had had their hands full with a travelling support which was much more than simply boisterous. "United supporters celebrated the Second Division title by turning Meadow Lane into a battlefield, after grabbing the points they needed for the Championship. Missiles were thrown, crash barriers broken and windows smashed as County were left counting the damage after United's 6,000 champion fans ran amok," wrote Turner. Another report said of the first half, "Crowd violence continued and huge lengths of wood ripped from emergency barriers at the Manchester United end of the ground were being used as weapons against police. One hundred officers lined the route behind the goal at the United end and dozens of Manchester fans were led away while others were carried on stretchers. Police dogs were sent in to the crowd in an attempt to stop the fighting." Seats were broken, windows were smashed and the Press Box ruined as Reds supporters caused an alleged £3,000 worth of damage - forty were arrested as another report said the club had been 'disgraced by their fans'.

Despite relinquishing a two goal lead, there was no disgrace on the pitch. Docherty insisted the second half performance was simply a consequence of the tiredness of his players after their international exploits. Still, Martin Buchan wasn't satisfied. "Of course we are delighted to lift the championship. But we should have done it in much better style," said the captain. "We had a two-goal lead at half time and then struggled badly in the second half. I can't understand how we suddenly lost form." Buchan insisted that the players would put it right on the final day. "There'll be no worries, no pressures then and we'll be going out to enjoy ourselves against Blackpool."

These were the immediate post-match reflections of the captain. Now, the crowd troubles of the game are his freshest memories. "I can't remember too much about crowd trouble at individual games although the Notts County game when we clinched the league stands out," he says. "During the last 5 or 6 minutes, they had a corner kick. It must have been at our end, because I rarely went up for them. There was a hell of a skirmish behind the goal with the supporters and you could barely concentrate about what was happening on the field because of the battle that was going on. There was crowd trouble at a lot of games, though, not just United, and the numbers we took meant there was more scope for trouble and, of course, adverse publicity. After the Notts County match we went to a club called Heart of the Midland which was owned by Joe Pullen, who also owned Talk of the North in Manchester. Joe was a friend of Les Olive, the club secretary, and we had a celebration there after the game."

United were back among the elite and were preparing for life accordingly. An around the world post-season tour had been announced that would take in the Far East and Australia, and in the week following the game at Notts County, plans were announced for the building of an 'Executive Club' which would hold 300 supporters. For £125 a season, they would have the service of their own restaurant in the South Stand - then referred to as the Main Stand. It was a £3 million project which included the removal of the pillars and installation of a cantilever stand to give a full, interrupted panoramic view of the pitch and arena.

The club's performances hadn't convinced everyone. Where some saw thrills and a competitive division, others saw mistakes, complacency and profligacy. The failure to put teams away was not down to United's missed chances, but an opinion that they weren't good enough. Norman Wynne was one such journalist. "There is a growing feeling that the team will not do credit to its surroundings," he wrote.

One could predict Docherty's response. "Rubbish," he scoffed. "This is what certain critics would like to see rather than what they honestly feel. Our record this season proves we can do well in the First Division. We beat Manchester City, Burnley and Middlesbrough in the League Cup and they have all been up with the leaders. So if that doesn't prove our worth I don't know what does. We are the best footballing side in the Second Division and the way we play we will lose goals because we let other teams play. But we have proved we've got the best record because we have put the emphasis on attacking football. And I give you this pledge: we will play the same way next season because that is the only way we can play. If we played the way Everton play there would be nobody here. Not a criticism. They play to their strengths. We cannot play that way. But there are critics who just don't want United to do well. If you want to look for shadows in any team you will find them. We've got our faults, we know that. But our players are 60 games older now and we have had a lot of pressure on us which we won't have next season."

Docherty said that he planned to have a look at some of the younger players ahead of the final game with Blackpool. "Now we have won the title we will give some youngsters a chance. What this club needs is a couple of years for these youngsters to mature," he said.

Clearly keen to shrug off any negativity, Docherty was keen to urge United supporters to concentrate on the positives of their support rather than condemn them for their actions in Nottingham. "It is easy enough to follow a winning team, but last season's League average of 42,712 during the fight for our First Division lives was tremendous," he wrote in his final programme notes for the 1974/75 season. "And even when we were doomed for the drop they did not leave us because that was about the figure for our opening few games in the Second Division. Since then, when it became clear we meant business, the crowds have risen to an average of nearly 48,000. I am sure that the gate will be over 50,000 for our final home appearance. I hope so because I want to take this opportunity of speaking to as many of you as possible when I offer a sincere thank you on behalf of the club for your tremendously loyal and encouraging support. It has definitely been one of the important factors that has spurred the team on in their bid for promotion. The players are always conscious that it is not just the manager they have to please... there is a huge following that is entitled to ask for nothing but the best and certainly demand a hundred per cent effort. We intend to try and express our appreciation from the pitch this afternoon. The players, the directors and the staff want you to know we appreciate the part you have played in the past and will play in the future towards making this fine club strong and successful again. I would add that we just as earnestly beg you not to let your excitement run away with you. Please do nothing silly or violent because we also want the reputation of our supporters to match the achievement of the players you have supported so well through thick and thin!"

Brian Greenhoff runs the gauntlet of a delighted Red Army after winning the championship at Meadow Lane

Saturday 26th April - Division Two - Old Trafford (58,769)

MANCHESTER UNITED 4-0 BLACKPOOL

Stepney, Forsyth, Houston, Greenhoff[1], James, Buchan, Coppell, McIlroy, Pearson[2], Macari[1], Daly

Having suggested that he would make changes, Docherty's United were in fact unchanged for the final day. As well as meaning kids like McCreery and Nicholl missed out on a chance to play, it also meant that Willie Morgan – last seen illuminating the left wing against Fulham – was not able to get a chance to say 'farewell' to Old Trafford.

SPECIAL SOUVENIR ISSUE
UNITED REVIEW *The official programme of Manchester United Football Club Ltd*
MANCHESTER UNITED v BLACKPOOL
26th April, 1975   Kick-off 3-00 p.m.   No. 28
SECOND DIVISION CHAMPIONS
SEASON 1974-1975
8p

Far from the organised events that take place these days with Queen blaring out over the public address system, the presentation of the Second Division Championship and the players' medals actually took place before the game. A lap of honour then followed the presentation in front of almost 60,000 supporters who once again represented the highest crowd in England that day (and, according to all accounts, there were a further 20,000 locked out), confirming that United could once more boast the highest average attendance in the country despite their second tier status. Their average of 48,389 was almost two and a half thousand more than Liverpool and they were promised by Docherty that "This is only the beginning!"

Seventh placed Blackpool came to Old Trafford with memories of their thrashing in the return still fresh in the memory and the newly crowned Champions set about bettering what many considered to be their best performance of the season. The swagger was prominent from front to back; Pearson scored in the 20th minute to set the celebrations really to life – John Burridge fumbled a free kick, and United's lead marksman was there to prod the ball in. The goalkeeper was at fault again early in the second half,

United's pre-match lap of honour

failing to hold a McIlroy effort, and Pearson was Johnny-on-the-spot again. He almost got a hat-trick in the 78th minute but United still benefitted - once more, Burridge was unable to keep hold of the ball. Less than five minutes later and it was four - Brian Greenhoff's close range effort rounding things off nicely.

From that point, it was

Stuart Pearson scores the opening goal

full on party mode. Even Steve James was described by Ronald Crowther as 'setting up scoring moves in Beckenbauer style'. Blackpool were barely interested in the game and it seemed that supporters were anxious for the final whistle so that they could get on the pitch and celebrate with their heroes. Referee Bill Gow blew for time a minute early, maybe to give the players an opportunity to get to safety, but it was a fruitless attempt as fans flooded the Old Trafford playing surface.

Memories of the season are, by and large, fond, but within the team there was more than just an element of embarrassment by the celebrations on this day. As overjoyed as they were to be returning to the top flight, the overriding feeling was that a wrong had been corrected, rather than something being accomplished. Macari said afterwards, "I couldn't get to the dressing room quickly enough," while Brian Greenhoff would later go on record as completely

Brian Greenhoff celebrates in the Directors' Box after the game

disregarding the achievement. "I can tell you where my FA Cup medal is, but I have no idea where the one for the Second Division is. We shouldn't have been down there," he said. In the book "The Doc's Devils" it is noted that elements of the support were 'ambivalent' regarding the celebrations too. Still, the mood was far more pleasant and less vitriolic than the pitch invasion at the end of the previous season.

Looking back, Sammy McIlroy can see why Macari was underwhelmed. "I see the point in that. Lou especially was one of those lads who came in with a big reputation and for someone like him it would have been a tragedy had we not gone up," he says. "Having said that, we still had to play, we still had to beat teams, and beat them well... that was the way at United. Expectations were high and higher still because of the way at the club. Perhaps because we were flying right from the start and it was expected I can see that they might have thought it was an anti-climax but I always look back on that season with great joy and fondness because of the way we played. We certainly didn't scrape it. We played the way we wanted and did it well... I personally got back on my feet and feeling good about myself and contribution. It had been a long battle in my head and body and now instead of someone fighting for his future I was now a part of a team that was really enjoying itself. I don't think I was the only one, and that's why I look back on it so warmly."

Martin Buchan, too, was one of those unimpressed by the jubilation at the time but his stance has since softened. "Well, of course the fans should have celebrated. It'd have been odd if they didn't and it would have been strange if we didn't too," he admits. "I suppose feeling that way at the time was probably just out of relief that we'd gone straight back up. It was just job done as far as we were concerned."

United were back where they belonged and the chairman, Louis

Edwards, was keen to address the supporters in the programme. "United supporters everywhere will be delighted that the Club have won promotion back to Division One at the first attempt and this is a great moment for everyone connected with our Club," he wrote. "There is no doubt that relegation twelve months ago was a bitter pill for us all to swallow and it is very gratifying that we should get back so quickly... we now look forward to a return to Division One and are confident that we will continue to make progress. As our Manager says, it will take time to reach the top and we will not have to expect things to happen too quickly but the foundation is laid and the build-up will go on until success at the top level again comes to Old Trafford. I trust you will all have a most enjoyable summer and look forward to welcoming you back to Old Trafford next August."

WHAT COULD HAVE BEEN...

COLLECTIVELY AND INDIVIDUALLY, Manchester United were set for a bright future after their promotion. Tommy Docherty's penchant for bold declarations was at times contradicted by his, at times, reserved predictions for the success of his team. He had asked for two years to get United challenging again but by Christmas Day 1975 they were top of Division One.

Docherty had also said that he would have much preferred to have spent his rebuilding period in mid-table but looking back, it is difficult to come to the conclusion that it would have had anywhere near the same effect. Confidence and momentum play such a crucial role psychologically, as does the atmosphere of a crowd on any given day. When you take every individual component, then ability, though it's undoubtedly the key factor, is just one attribute in a number that help to determine results and, consequently, form.

It has already been mentioned Morgan and McIlroy were outstanding dribblers but they were not George Best - Lou Macari was well capable of scoring goals but he wasn't Denis Law - and Brian Greenhoff, as well as he did in his first season, was not the Bobby Charlton he was being hyped to be. That is not to say that each of those four players did not bring immense qualities to the team and such is the rationale that to look at each of the players over their careers then certainly in the case of Law and Charlton you could not have asked them to do what Macari and Greenhoff eventually went on to contribute. Law worked hard but was a predator rather than a midfield hustler. Charlton was the heart of the 1968 team but where he was so reliable in front of goal and Greenhoff wasn't, similarly, Greenhoff was a capable defender and it's difficult to imagine Charlton being as composed as a centre half.

But in 1974, these were the comparisons being made, and the struggles which the players had to deal with. When George Best left the club for the final time in January 1974, it was a significant moment in the history of the club - confidence went into freefall, the players felt lost, and with self-doubt infecting all corners of Old Trafford including the manager, relegation became an inevitability. Only when all hope was lost did Docherty finally just say (after encouragement from Sir Matt Busby), 'To hell with it', and wanted United to go down fighting. This too was an important moment as it meant the players faced the drop, when it came, not with their heads down, but positive about the way that they had ended the season.

The 'Doc' may well have wished to not be stigmatised as the man who took Manchester United into Division Two but what good would have surviving by the skin of their teeth done to his players' confidence?

One could argue that instead of being a brilliant manager, Docherty got lucky with a few forced calls that just turned out to be masterstrokes. Moving Greenhoff to defence because Steve James was injured and switching to 4-2-4 to accommodate Morgan and McIlroy. Lucky? Okay, but as the saying goes, you earn your luck, and Docherty had earned that luck on this occasion by sticking with the philosophy that Manchester United are cavalier and will attack. He had learned from his cautiousness.

If we were being flippant then we could argue that relegation was Docherty's best ever mistake. Had United remained in the top flight, they would have been of the collective belief that they were in their natural position. That was where they deserved to be. And what would the goal have been for the following season? Gradual improvement, perhaps? Maybe the attitude to prove themselves better than what they had showed in the '73/74 season, but what would have happened after two or three bad results?

In Division Two there was an expectation after a blow to the collective pride of the group. All accepted responsibility for the part they played, though it may well have been down to the fact that there had been no obvious replacement for the 'Holy Trinity' and nobody had stepped up to the mark. When they had left, they were all past their peak but the symbolic nature of how and when everything happened was damaging to a team that were shorn of this natural ability. It was a necessary change but a transition that was understandably extremely difficult for such a young team to deal with, particularly those brought through by Docherty. It should be taken into consideration of course that the manager felt that with a little more time in the season he could have kept United up. It's not a leap from logic to conclude that he felt the momentum generated by that end of season run could be carried into the next campaign (as of course was proven by the return to Division One when it did arrive).

Alex Forsyth was one of the first men Docherty signed, for the princely sum of £100,000, but he only really became a fixture in the side in January 1974, right in the midst of United's darkest hour. Greenhoff had been introduced into the side in September 1973 after a few years going through the reserves and youth teams. Stewart Houston had signed for the club in 1973, Lou Macari was an expensive gamble from the manager, while after a couple of years of his career stalling, Sammy McIlroy was concerned for his own future. All six would play crucial roles in Division Two but could be said to have fragile confidences in the summer of

1974. Aside from McIlroy, that list of players were all Doc's boys, players that the manager had to continue to show faith in to turn it around. In return, they were determined to do so.

"The lads had so much determination to get out of the division," says McIlroy. "There was no way we'd have taken second best. The crowd wanted to know that we were 100% committed and once they did the support was absolutely unbelievable. We were favourites from the get go. We were going to grounds we'd never been before and I actually started the season playing up front alongside Pancho - we had a great understanding. I was a sub on the first day against Orient, before then breaking in to the side and kicking on. We knew what we would come up against but our only objective was to go and attack every team we played, home or away. We had a fantastic start, beating teams for fun, and the media enjoyed it too - we were like a runaway train, so confident home or away."

The expectancy for the players to perform and the prestige with which they were treated by opponents was essentially an imitation of the halcyon days that the club had gloriously lived so recently. Had they remained in the top flight, while still the 'biggest' scalp, United would simply have been seen as faded stars, and in that respect, psychologically this feeling may have been transferred on to players. In the Second Division, they were the target and the red carpet was rolled out for them.

The momentum generated from that early run of good results earned United an unassailable five point advantage and from that point on, the confidence grew, save for a temporary dip in form in the winter. The change in mood was reflected by the manager just before Christmas when he was confident enough to say his team would be promoted.

And far from costing them their careers, the year in Division Two was the making of some. Lou Macari might have had his nose put out of joint by the signing of Stuart Pearson but as the season wore on he became more and more important, with his all action performances and endurance vital. United had found resilience in their opposition and so it took the perseverance of Macari to help break sides down – this was never more evident than over Easter Weekend.

Others had more profound problems. Sammy McIlroy suffered a car crash in January 1973 and that meant he missed the rest of Docherty's first season in charge. Though he was reassured by his manager that he'd get a chance, he spent a lot of time in the 1973/74 season with Brian Kidd, who was unhappy that he was out of favour with the manager. With his contract up at the end of that season, and United relegated, McIlroy was probably justified in the self-doubt he has already confessed to. As it was, he would later describe relegation as 'the best thing to ever happen to us' and he might as well have been speaking about himself as much as the team because he went from strength to strength, finally coming out of the shadow of others and proving himself a vital member of the attack with his penetration. Yet now, he is undecided about his earlier comment. "Though there were positive consequences, relegation can never be considered a good thing," says McIlroy. "For me you can't consider the hypothetical situations of what might have been if we had survived and not gone down. We had to get back as soon as possible but the pleasing thing was how we did it. Still, relegation for Manchester United is a tragedy... it worked out well, and the confidence we got and the team that was build in the aftermath was good, but it should never have gotten to that."

Arguably the only player whose stock was high going into the season was Brian Greenhoff, and, ironically enough, he was the one player who openly admitted complacency in his own form early in the season. It recovered sufficiently that his place in the team was never really in question, but it could be argued that while his versatility meant he was near enough always guaranteed a place in the side, the lack of a settled position didn't help him find his best form. It's no surprise that that came when he was finally given a full time role at centre half.

Alex Stepney, as the unlikely goalscoring hero, also came into the Second Division with his reputation fairly safe, as did Martin Buchan. As the latter came out of the 1974/75 season with the captain's armband and his place at the club secure, the former had found his place vulnerable for the first time in his United career. Stepney would be dropped again the following season by Docherty and replaced by Roche on four occasions. In fact, on the eve of the following season, Stepney had been told he would be back up goalkeeper, only for the death of Roche's father the night before the opening game to throw that back into the air.

Long term, Docherty had planned to bring in another goalkeeper, with Peter Shilton his prime target. Edwards refused to back his manager with the money – and Shilton went to Nottingham Forest. A number of players, including Greenhoff and later, Gordon Hill, would go on record to say that if United had signed Shilton, they'd have won the league and possibly a European Cup. Again, it's all ifs and buts, yet looking at Forest's success in the years to come, it's a logical conclusion to make. That is not to say that Stepney was a bad goalkeeper. Far from it. But at almost 33, he was past his peak, and it was logical for the manager to look for areas in which to improve his team. Stepney remained at the club until 1978 – outlasting Docherty after enjoying FA Cup success with him.

Some believe a better goalkeeper would have proved the difference between United finishing as Champions and in third place in 1976 (they were four points behind Liverpool). Others think they should have won it anyway. Martin Buchan says he 'will go to his grave' believing that the FA Cup run proved an unwelcome distraction. He has a point. United had lost just one league game in 18 prior to the semi final against Derby County. They were three points behind QPR and Liverpool, but had two games in hand. Afterwards, they lost three in five, which proved to be what did for their chances.

Brian Greenhoff agreed with his captain. "As much as I'd like to think we didn't take our eye off the ball, everything was so hectic with all the Cup Final coverage and suit measuring that we couldn't help but have our attention diverted," he admitted.

And while the goalkeeper couldn't be blamed for any of the three defeats, it's worth pointing out that the defeat to Stoke City was one that should have been a win but for the visiting keeper being in inspired form. His name? Peter Shilton. "I dare say I'm not the only one who looks back at that Stoke game with disappointment," said Gordon Hill.

Another player with the Second Division to thank for his United career is Stuart Pearson, who might well have never played for the club at all had they not been relegated. After all, to again work on a logical assumption that had they survived in 1974, the players would need some kind of figurehead, then Docherty may well have gone for a big name to appease supporters. He might have gone in for Peter Osgood, a player he had attempted to sign at the tail end of the relegation season. He might have kept Kidd. He probably wouldn't have been backed to gamble with Pearson, considering Hull were perennial mid-table finishers in the second tier. 'Pancho', an experienced Second Division forward, was able to grow into the role of a Manchester United forward to the extent that by the time it came to play in Division One, he was as confident as the rest of his team mates. This is conjecture of course and the Doc insists that Pearson was a sure thing, indicating that he may well have gone for him if United had stayed up.

If the above players were the solid structure, a Red machine that moved, defended and attacked as one, then Steve Coppell and Gordon Hill were the jewels in the crown. Hill was to follow later on – still a relative gamble by Docherty, but one that the manager had earned after the overwhelming success with Coppell who was seemingly a natural in United's number seven jersey. Would Docherty have been able to sign Coppell, throwing him right into the first team at the expense of Willie Morgan, while allowing him to train only once a week while he completed his studies, in the unforgiving spotlight of the First Division? Not a chance.

Martin Buchan later referred to Coppell as "the best player in that 1975/76 side", and elaborating on that for this record, said, "When people ask me who the best player I ever played with at United was, well, from what I consider to be my United team, then I would say Steve Coppell. By a mile. He was so refreshing. He was only part time when he first joined, but for me he became the most valuable player of the Tommy Doc era, and it was a tragedy that he lost his career at such a young age." The winger ,who had had a pending payment for twenty appearances, went on to make 396 but was forced to retire with injury at the age of 28, he was surely destined to finish in the top ten appearance makers for the club until that point.

It's natural to wonder about the potential of that side as it was so great – and these are simply this writer's thoughts. The difference in opinion makes for great debate, though it can be universally accepted that the team never quite reached the levels it seemed capable of after Docherty's sacking in July 1977.

A question which is more pertinent and relevant to this particular record is whether or not relegation was a good thing for Manchester United. According to the manager, no, according to several of the players, it was the best thing that could have happened (even if McIlroy, on later reflection, appears undecided on that). We are back to the 'what if's - the 'pointless' hypotheticals - if we are to guess what might have happened had the club survived in the top flight but working on the logical paths that each player followed and the positive effects the setbacks had on careers that may otherwise have stalled and faded then how can any conclusion other than relegation was overwhelmingly positive for the club, be reached?

And perhaps it's with that common consensus, that so many supporters remember that season so fondly. Like Lou Macari says, it is probably a combination of things. Travelling to new places, seeing their team win and entertain, but more than that, seeing the team develop and grow together. McIlroy agrees. "It's remembered, simply, for the football," he says. "To play attacking football, to come straight back up, scoring plenty of goals... all of it. For myself, the Sunderland game sticks out, as well as the final game against Blackpool with thousands locked out. I still remember the Norwich game in the League Cup as a strong memory from that season because it was so disappointing to lose out. It rankles. I don't care what anyone says, it's always great to play at Wembley, every players' dream in the Seventies and of course we hadn't been there since 1968."

Like Macari, McIlroy confesses that the reason that players share the fondness that supporters feel for the '74/75 season is in part due to the fact that it was when they really began to find their feet - and that is because they were allowed to. How often do you see teams relegated, and the players instantly sold because they either weren't good enough or they were poached by a bigger club? United were, of course, in the unique position that it was still Docherty's decision ultimately to sell Brian Kidd rather than the player force a move, but it is still to his credit that by and large, he gave most of the players a chance to make amends. With such a young average age in the outfield, it would have been easy to discard these players as simply not good enough, but their manager had the nous to appreciate the damage that lack of self-belief can do.

Disregarding the temptation to continue to explore the unknown, the obvious point to make is that the story went on. The events of 1974/75 continued to influence the club in the modern era, throughout the rest of Docherty's reign and beyond. The repercussions of the relegation (although, more accurately, we should acknowledge this as the positive repercussions of promotion) influenced Manchester United's immediate future.

So, too, did the hooligan culture. It wasn't confined to United supporters and it didn't magically end in 1975. It could not be said that it was the only thing that caused the reaction but in acknowledging the pitch invasion which followed the City game in April 1974, the fences which were erected at Old Trafford became common place at football grounds. The death of a football supporter at Blackpool early in the season was the catalyst for the segregation of supporters, and as we observed at points throughout the 1974/75 season, at times, the 'all-ticket' approach and confining supporters to one section of the ground wasn't always as well planned as it had been hoped.

United as a club seemed to do everything that they could do to comply. They agreed to the request to install fences; Docherty himself went on record in the national, local and club press to urge supporters to behave. The players arranged meetings with supporters to try and persuade them to act in an orderly fashion. There has to be more than just a smidgeon of truth in the belief that Second Division clubs and the local police and authorities were simply unprepared for the hordes of United supporters. It was unprecedented, so how could they have been expected to know?

However unsavoury the scenes at Old Trafford on April 27th, 1974, they were nothing compared to what happened at White Hart Lane on April 19th, 1975. Tottenham Hotspur and Chelsea faced off in a televised head to head where the losers faced relegation to the Second Division. There were numerous pitch invasions - fights on the pitch and terraces, trouble outside the ground. There was disturbing footage during one pitch invasion of a crowd of hooligans chasing an individual, knocking him to the ground and then attacking him further. Some watched horrified, realising it had gone too far.

More shame was to follow for English football. Leeds United had recovered from their poor start under Brian Clough and even though they finished a disappointing 9th in Division One under Jimmy Armfield, they reached the European Cup Final to take on German giants Bayern Munich (who themselves had finished a lowly 10th in their domestic league). A brutal game which was packed with fouls - Frank Gray's challenge on Uli Hoeneß would end the German's career, while Leeds were outraged at the failure of the referee to award a penalty. A Leeds goal in the 67th minute was controversially disallowed, causing rioting on the stands. When Bayern scored five minutes later, Leeds supporters couldn't control themselves and began to destroy the Parc des Princes stands they were housed in, throwing debris on the pitch. Leeds players were unsettled by the behaviour of their own fans, Bayern scored again, and French riot place came into the stadium - they were unable to prevent the Yorkshire supporters from trashing Paris. Subsequently, Leeds were banned from European football for four seasons, becoming the first English club to suffer a suspension from continental competition, though on appeal, that was reduced to two.

In the interests of balance, after United qualified for the European Cup Winners' Cup in 1977, their behaviour in France against Saint Etienne was punished by being kicked out of the competition. They were re-instated, but were ordered to play their home game in the return leg in a venue 200km from Old Trafford. They chose Plymouth's Home Park.

Even after the ban for all English clubs in Europe, and after their reinstatement, there has still been trouble at times. Where there are large numbers of people indulging in a drinking culture, it is an unsavoury but inevitable consequence that there will be some trouble.

The players have their own individual feelings on it, but Martin Buchan's opinion that despite the trouble, they never felt particularly threatened, is shared more or less by all.

"We played at full houses every match that season and it's always good to know whether they're shouting for or against you," he says. "One of my outstanding memories is playing for Scotland against Spain at Valencia. Spain never had a national stadium, they moved their games about, but when they needed to win games, they played them at the Mestalla because it was very compact. The crowd were right on top of you. There must have been 60,000 shouting Spaniards and 500 Scots, but what an atmosphere, it made you play. Even a hostile atmosphere makes you play. There was never too much hostility for us in that season in Division Two. I was never frightened, I never felt in physical danger, but the Notts County game is the one that stands out. We played at Millwall on a Monday and I can't imagine that that was too friendly an atmosphere but it doesn't really stick out. Maybe because it was early in the season."

Arnie Sidebottom's reflections mirror his former team-mates – while not quite trivialising the issues, portraying them in a different light. "We'd take over the grounds. It'd be red and white wherever we went, it felt like every match was a home match. It neutralised the hostility from the players that we'd get," he says.

In the grand scheme of things, the hooligan problem that dogged United's 1974/75 season was pretty much on par for how things were in English football that year. It's not an excuse, but there are at least the aforementioned circumstances that have to be taken into consideration.

For those who travelled to away games in 1974/75, there are special memories that are unlikely to ever be replicated, at least not for a couple of generations. Away games at Anfield and Goodison Park generate hostile atmospheres, while Arsenal and Manchester City are decidedly more sterile in their new arenas compared to the days of Highbury and Maine Road. These are journeys made year upon year, familiar journeys and routines even if the anticipation of memories to be created is fresh and exciting. As mentioned earlier in this record, supporters hope for far flung, random away games in the Cup for the experience of seeing something new.

It is natural for misty-eyed and nostalgic fans to recall the team they watched in their adolescence as their heroes. Some are all too aware of the tendency of nostalgia to cloud the mind. "I think the season is very fondly remembered by me and my contemporaries as like with most things of a bygone age, things always seemed better, also after two or three years of almost continually losing United were actually winning, albeit in a lower division," admits Gary Thompson. "I don't think that mattered much to us though. My interpretation of the team was that the bulk of that Second Division side went on to take the First Division by storm the following season and also won the FA Cup. How good could they have become? That's a tough one given Liverpool's dominance of the time. Had the Doc not been sacked I could have foreseen several more Cups, but the league? I'm not so sure."

The very young average age of Docherty's 1975 team made them all the more likeable to impressionable fans. The swagger and style which returned to the club throughout that year was very much a rebirth. Supporters who were between the age of 10 and 15 during this season, therefore, will likely always regard this team as one of their very favourites regardless of the fact that they only went on to win the FA Cup. In some ways, the fact that they were dismantled before fulfilling their collective potential makes them all the more romantic. Nevertheless Sammy McIlroy believes that they were on the cusp of greatness, "Everyone joined in on our team, attacking and defensively, there were no shirkers. With maybe one or two additions we would have won the League with that Cup Final side in 1977. You might laugh but Barcelona's recent teams were so successful because as soon as they lost the ball they got it back. We were doing that in the 70's under Tommy Doc and Tommy Cavanagh. We harried people, got in their faces, we'd toe-poke balls away, make them pass the ball as quickly as possible to create mistakes. Everyone talks about how fit the Barcelona team are but we were doing the same and the energy levels were unbelievable in our side."

It's a thought echoed by Brian Greenhoff in his 2012 autobiography. "We played at a hundred miles an hour, a philosophy that others had described as a high offside trap but we always simply called 'attack the ball'. It was a prototype of the pressing game that Barcelona and Spain have perfected recently. Our strength was going forward. It wasn't easy having defenders under six foot against strikers well over, so we used to turn it around and try and play in their half instead, which is something we did very well. I suppose we were ahead of our time in many respects."

Captain Martin Buchan is another on the list who shares the feeling that there should have been more success and that there probably would have been. "I just wish he'd been able to stay after our 1977 Cup Final victory against Liverpool because we'll never know how good that team could have been," Buchan remembers. "I always thought we could have done better in that first season back in the First Division. We were distracted by the FA Cup. The lads thought they'd be millionaires with the players' pool and believe me, a few of them got their heads turned. They thought they'd just turn up against Southampton and get a medal. Well they did, but a loser's one. Because of that distraction our league form suffered. In other circumstances we could have won that league. The midfield we had didn't have a cruncher or a ball winner. But they didn't let you rest. If they didn't win the ball by nicking it, they forced errors in possession. There was not a team better in the country at doing that than us.

"We had two footballers in the back four after Jim's injury, two players comfortable on the ball. The following year we won the Cup with a great contribution from Jimmy Greenhoff, who I always say was Tommy Doc's Eric Cantona, because he was the one who brought other people into play. He was the catalyst for what we achieved and what we should have - but we'll never know if we could have built on that. He'd been after Peter Shilton, although for me there was nothing wrong with Alex Stepney, who was almost thirty-five, and was seldom injured. Everyone said Peter was worth ten points a season. Maybe if he'd have done that, I might well have been replaced by Colin Todd. Who knows? Although I had my moments with him and we had our ups and downs, the times I had with Doc were the happiest days of my playing career. He cleared out a lot of the deadwood and rebuilt the squad... I played with Best, Law and Charlton, and I can tell my grandkids that I played alongside those three on that wonderful statue outside Old Trafford. They are symbols of Manchester United. I joined United in 1972, four years after they won the European Cup. But that wasn't my era... I regard my era as when Doc rebuilt the team. I have great memories of them but my team, my Manchester United, was the one from those days under Doc with Steve Coppell, Sammy McIlroy, Lou Macari, Gerry Daly and Gordon Hill buzzing in midfield and on the wing, and Brian alongside me in defence."

It is a step too far to compare the lost collective potential to those who perished in Munich but for young supporters in 1977, when Tommy Docherty was sacked, they were faced with the loss of another young side. For football romantics of a certain age there remains a desire to pontificate over the potential of this Manchester United team. Before concerning ourselves with the reality of what befell them, let us first indulge in what might have been.

First of all, it is worthwhile to consider an anecdote often uttered by Gordon Hill, that Bill Shankly warned his team that 'that lot down the M62 are coming' after the 1977 FA Cup Final. Liverpool had just been defeated, with United ending their hopes of a treble, ahead of their European Cup Final victory in Rome. Shankly's words were probably intended to motivate his own players but Gordon Hill, for one, insists there was more than a modicum of truth to them. How realistic is it to suggest that United might have rivalled Liverpool as the premier team in the country during the next decade and, perhaps, on the continent, too?

United's average age in that FA Cup Final was approximately 23 - including veterans Alex Stepney and Jimmy Greenhoff. Let us consider that squad as a collective was yet to reach its physical peak with accepted wisdom that such a peak would have been three years afterwards. With a six-year spell together, had Docherty been in charge, their natural decline may have started around 1982 or 1983.

A look at the league winners from that time show that it is not as easy as saying United would have overtaken Liverpool after the Cup Final because the Anfield side won the League title five times in the next 8 season to add to their successes in 1976 and 1977.

The matter becomes less straightforward by initially considering that first year back. The players of that era still lament the defeat to Stoke City on 21st April 1976. The pain is still visible on the faces of Sammy McIlroy, Martin Buchan and Gordon Hill if you mention that game to them. Peter Shilton's heroics in goal for Stoke that day are emphatically more pronounced simply because he was linked with a move to United before the start of the season and the fact that just about everyone at Old Trafford (except, of course, for Alex Stepney) wanted him at the club.

Of course, there is no guarantee that Shilton's presence at United would have made any difference but it is a reasonable enough theory that a world class keeper such as him would have had an impact. United lost their next game, to Leicester City, and those defeats turned into wins would have seen them level on points with Liverpool. They would have still been behind on goal average, which then highlights the potential benefit of having Shilton in goal all season. In the interest of fairness and balance, however, it's worth pointing out that United under Docherty would still play at full throttle, so may still have at times endured some fragility at the back.

Shilton's name is not only intriguing because of the team he played for and the part he played in April 1976 but because of the team he later signed for and the success they would go on to enjoy. In fact it is that circumstance more than any other which provokes the real substance behind the 'what if?' because Clough's embryonic Nottingham Forest had finished 16th in Division Two in 1974/75. By 1978 Forest, with Shilton in goal, were Division One champions and in 1979 and 1980 they won back to back European Cups. Aston Villa, promoted in 1974/75 under Ron Saunders were Division One champions in 1981 and won the European Cup (under Tony Barton) in 1982.

It would be insulting the intelligence to suggest that United were simply a Shilton away from winning all of that treasure in place of Forest and Villa. He would certainly have made an upgrade on United prior to 1977 and could well have tipped the 1976 Division One title race in their favour but even so, the team that won the FA Cup in 1977 had a far greater potential than was realised.

What went wrong?

Clearly, the turning point was the dismissal of Tommy Docherty. Whether this was a decision forced on the United board is a question for another day (there's no doubt that Docherty had his enemies at boardroom level) but it was still, in purely football terms, a decision that prompted instant regression, ruling United out of contention to capitalise on any transition period Liverpool were to go through.

Docherty had built an intensely loyal core of players and he had managed to establish them as a side feared by everyone in the country, on any ground, because they aimed for a win wherever they went. It is not often a club has all the ingredients in place, ready for imminent success, but even if the board defend their decision to relieve Docherty of their duties on moral grounds, in hindsight there is little doubt that it was the wrong decision for the advancement of the team. The chemistry was perfect and the Doc was the right man to know what to do to springboard them from the platform of FA Cup success.

Dave Sexton was brought in having been identified as the manager of tomorrow but his quiet and pensive personality was not received well by many of the players. Ironically, those accusations of dishonesty which had been levelled against Docherty by former players and even at boardroom level were repeated against Sexton from two of the key players of that side, Brian Greenhoff and Gordon Hill. The two serve as significant figures in the ensuing transition.

It should be pointed out that it ought to be expected that any new manager will have his own ideas and it was as much the fault of the board to sack Docherty and identify Sexton as the suitable successor as it was that of Sexton to change the club's playing style. Sexton's preference was to have a more uncompromising centre half and more defensively-minded wide men – it was a systematic dissection, ripping the heart out of all that was adored by United. This is no disservice to Sexton's choice of players to come in – Gordon McQueen and Mickey Thomas who are still so highly respected at the club for their own contributions that they frequently appear through the club's various media channels – but their differing qualities, and Sexton's preferred style of play, forced a significant change from the breathless Manchester United style that football supporters all over the country had fallen in love with over the previous three seasons.

It is also significant that the numbers watching the club fell from an average of 53,000 at Old Trafford and 35,000 away from home in 1976/77 to 46,000 and 30,000 respectively by 1978/79 – so it wasn't only United fans who were turned off by the change, supporters of all stripes preferred gung-ho Docherty to pragmatic Sexton. By 1977, Greenhoff had established himself in the heart of defence alongside Buchan. He had not matured into the world class midfielder that had been predicted in 1974 but he had brought something not seen before to United's defence, a first class distributor of the ball and an excellent reader of the game – more Beckenbauer than Charlton.

Gordon McQueen brought different qualities – an undoubtedly greater physical presence (though the worth of Greenhoff's heart and resilience ought not to be discounted) and a threat in the opposition penalty area from corners. However, all good teams build from the back, and United suffered from the loss of the chemistry which had been created. Eventually, after being played in a number of different positions, Greenhoff was sold to Leeds for a then club record fee.

Gordon Hill's future at the club was resolved far sooner. Signed in September 1976 Hill became essential to United's counter-attack play. No assessment of the potential of Docherty's team would be complete without Hill. Gordon was transferred to Derby County in April 1978. This move (coincidentally to join up with his old manager Docherty at the Baseball Ground) was symbolic and underlined the profound difference between Sexton's United and the one he had inherited. Mickey Thomas was capable of the occasionally brilliant as opposed to the regularly jaw-dropping – Hill, when sold, was the club's top scorer, from the left wing.

Gordon Hill was part of the reason many feel the club could have competed on the continental stage. He scored a tremendous volley against Juventus in the 1976-77 UEFA Cup Second Round which was enough to earn United a one goal victory at Old Trafford after a well earned success over Ajax in the previous round. They were eliminated by eventual winners Juventus in Turin but it is worth pointing out that their opposition in European competition that season was far more formidable than that which Liverpool faced on their way to winning the European Cup.

Returning to the theme of transfers. Let us speculate that United would, under Docherty, have finished as champions in 1978, instead of Forest. That prestige would have seen them in a favourable position to compete for the better players and it is such an argument, which isn't totally unreasonable, which makes

By season's end, The Doc had put a smile back on the faces of United supporters

it feasible that the Reds could have been in the position they eventually enjoyed in 1993 some 15 years sooner. Admittedly, this would have been well before the game enjoyed (or suffered, depending on your point of view) the financial injection from the boom of the Premier League. Yet there was no secret that Docherty was intent on restoring the club to the glamorous heights of 1968. He would probably have had to contend with the purse strings still being tight, but then, this was a problem about which Ferguson often complained, and he was still permitted a summer or six of lavish spending.

Still, all we are left with is speculation. Ask the players and supporters of the time, and they will tell you that the Manchester United team that was promoted to Division One in 1975 was as exciting and as packed with potential as any other in the club's history. That they failed to achieve their potential is one of the great what if's in English football history.

BIBLIOGRAPHY

The following publications were referenced when putting this book together.

"Manchester United - The Forgotten Fixtures" by Iain McCartney

"The Doc's Devils" by Sean Egan

"Call the Doc" by Tommy Docherty with Derek Henderson

"Alex Stepney" by Alex Stepney

"Tooting Common to the Stretford End" by Alex Stepney and David Saffer

"Wilf McGuinness - Man and Babe" by Wilf McGuinness and Ivan Ponting

"The Doc : My Story - Hallowed Be Thy Game" by Tommy Docherty.

Thanks to Tommy Docherty for kind permission to use his words and programme notes from *United Review* – The *United Review* from 1974/75 as well as the match programmes from all other 21 Division Two clubs have been referenced. Finally, *U-NITED*, the official newsletter from 1974/75, has been referenced.

REDS ON RECORD

MANCHESTER UNITED 1974/75

FOOTBALL LEAGUE DIVISION TWO

Date	Opponent	Score	Venue	Attendance	Scorers
Sat 17 Aug 1974	Orient	2-0	Brisbane Road	17,772	Houston, Macari
Sat 24 Aug 1974	MILLWALL	4-0	Old Trafford	44,756	Daly (3), Pearson
Wed 28 Aug 1974	PORTSMOUTH	2-1	Old Trafford	42,547	Daly, McIlroy
Sat 31 Aug 1974	Cardiff City	1-0	Ninian Park	22,344	Daly
Sat 07 Sep 1974	NOTTINGHAM FOREST	2-2	Old Trafford	40,671	Greenhoff, McIlroy
Sat 14 Sep 1974	West Bromwich Albion	1-1	The Hawthorns	23,721	Pearson
Mon 16 Sep 1974	Millwall	1-0	The Den (old)	16.988	Daly
Sat 21 Sep 1974	BRISTOL ROVERS	2-0	Old Trafford	42,948	Greenhoff, Prince (og)
Wed 25 Sep 1974	BOLTON WANDERERS	3-0	Old Trafford	47,084	Houston, Macari, McAllister (og)
Sat 28 Sep 1974	Norwich City	0-2	Carrow Road	24,586	
Sat 05 Oct 1974	Fulham	2-1	Craven Cottage	26,513	Pearson (2)
Sat 12 Oct 1974	NOTTS. COUNTY	1-0	Old Trafford	46,565	
Tue 15 Oct 1974	Portsmouth	0-0	Fratton Park	25,608	
Sat 19 Oct 1974	Blackpool	3-0	Bloomfield Road	25,370	Forsyth, Macari, McCalliog
Sat 26 Oct 1974	SOUTHAMPTON	1-0	Old Trafford	48,724	Pearson
Sat 02 Nov 1974	OXFORD UNITED	4-0	Old Trafford	41,909	Pearson (3), Macari
Sat 09 Nov 1974	Bristol City	0-1	Ashton Gate	28,104	
Sat 16 Nov 1974	ASTON VILLA	2-1	Old Trafford	55,615	Daly (2)
Sat 23 Nov 1974	Hull City	0-2	Boothferry Park	23,287	
Sat 30 Nov 1974	SUNDERLAND	3-2	Old Trafford	60,585	McIlroy, Morgan, Pearson
Sat 07 Dec 1974	Sheffield Wednesday	4-4	Hillsborough	35,230	Macari (2), Houston,. Pearson
Sat 14 Dec 1974	ORIENT	0-0	Old Trafford	41,200	
Sat 21 Dec 1974	York City	1-0	Bootham Crescent	15,567	Pearson
Thu 26 Dec 1974	WEST BROMWICH ALBION	2-1	Old Trafford	51,104	Daly, McIlroy
Sat 28 Dec 1974	Oldham Athletic	0-1	Boundary Park	26,384	
Sat 11 Jan 1975	SHEFFIELD WEDNESDAY	2-0	Old Trafford	45,662	McCalliog (2)
Sat 18 Jan 1975	Sunderland	0-0	Roker Park	45,976	
Sat 01 Feb 1975	BRISTOL CITY	0-1	Old Trafford	47,118	
Sat 08 Feb 1975	Oxford United	0-1	Manor Ground	15,959	
Sat 15 Feb 1975	HULL CITY	2-0	Old Trafford	44,712	Houston, Pearson
Sat 22 Feb 1975	Aston Villa	0-2	Villa Park	39,156	
Sat 01 Mar 1975	CARDIFF CITY	4-0	Old Trafford	43,601	Houston, McIlroy, Macari, Pearson
Sat 08 Mar 1975	Bolton Wanderers	1-0	Burnden Park	38,152	Pearson
Sat 15 Mar 1975	NORWICH CITY	1-1	Old Trafford	56,202	Pearson
Sat 22 Mar 1975	Nottingham Forest	1-0	City Ground	21,893	Daly
Fri 28 Mar 1975	Bristol Rovers	1-1	Eastville Stadium	19,337	Macari
Sat 29 Mar 1975	YORK CITY	2-1	Old Trafford	46,802	Macari, Morgan
Mon 31 Mar 1975	OLDHAM ATHLETIC	3-2	Old Trafford	56,618	Coppell, Macari, Morgan
Sat 05 Apr 1975	Southampton	1-0	The Dell	21,866	Macari
Sat 12 Apr 1975	FULHAM	1-0	Old Trafford	52,971	Daly
Sat 19 Apr 1975	Notts. County	2-2	Meadow Lane	17,320	Greenhoff, Houston
Sat 26 Apr 1975	BLACKPOOL	4-0	Old Trafford	58,769	Pearson (2), Greenhoff, Macari

LEAGUE CUP

Date	Round	Opponent	Score	Attendance	Scorers
11 Sept	R3	CHARLTON ATHLETIC	5-1	26,616	McIlroy, Macari (2), Houston, Daly (pen)
9 Oct	R4	MANCHESTER CITY	1-0	55,159	Daly (pen)
13 Nov	R5	BURNLEY	3-2	46,269	Morgan, Macari (2)
4 Dec	Q-F	Middlesbrough	0-0	36,005	
18 Dec	Q-F replay	MIDDLESBROUGH (REPLAY)	3-0	49,501	McIlroy, Pearson, Macari
15 Jan	S-F 1st leg	NORWICH CITY	2-1	58,010	Macari (2)
22 Jan	S-F 2nd leg	Norwich City	0-1	31,621	

FA CUP

Date	Round	Opponent	Score	Attendance	Scorers
4 Jan	R3	WALSALL	0-0	43,353	
7th Jan	R3 replay	Walsall	02-Mar	18,105	McIlroy. Daly (pen)

APPEARANCES AND GOALS

Player	League	League Cup	FA Cup	Total
McIlroy	41 (1), 7	2,1	7,2	50 (1), 10
Buchan	41,0	2,0	7,0	50,0
Stepney	40,0	2,0	7,0	49,0
Houston	40,6	2,0	6,1	48,7
Greenhoff	39 (2),4	2,0	6,0	47 (2),4
Daly	36 (1)	2,1	7,1	45 (1), 13
Forsyth	39,1	-	6,0	45,1
Macari	36 (2), 11	2,0	6 (1),7	44 (3), 18
Morgan	32 (2),3	1,0	6 (1),1	39 (3),4
Pearson	30 (1), 17	2,0	4,1	36 (1), 18
McCalliog	20,3	1,0	5 (1),0	26 (1),3
Holton	14,0	-	3,0	17,0
Sidebottom	12,0	2,0	2,0	16,0
James	13,0	-	2,0	15,0
Young	7 (8),0	2,0	1,(4)	10 (12),0
Coppell	9 (1),1	-	-	9 (1),1
Martin	7 (1),0	-	1,0	8 (1),0
Albiston	2,0	-	1,0	3,0
Baldwin	2,0	-	-	2,0
Roche	2,0	-	-	2,0
Davies	0 (8),0	0 (2),0	-	0 (10),0
McCreery	0 (2),0	-	-	0 (2),0
Graham	0 (1),0	-	-	0 (1),0
Nicholl	0 (1) ,0	-	-	0 (1),0

TOP 10 BEST SUPPORTED CLUBS - 1974/75

1. Manchester United	DIV. 2	48.389
2. Liverpool	DIV. 1	45.966
3. Everton	DIV. 1	40.021
4. Leeds United	DIV. 1	34.822
5. Newcastle United	DIV. 1	34.614
6. Manchester City	DIV. 1	32.898
7. Birmingham City	DIV. 1	30.854
8. Sunderland	DIV. 1	29.931
9. West Ham United	DIV. 1	29.872
10. Middlesbrough	DIV. 1	28.605

courtesy of www.european-football-statistics.co.uk

MANCHESTER UNITED LEAGUE ATTENDANCES 1974/75

HOME - TOTAL 1,290,087 - AVERAGE 47,781

AWAY - TOTAL 616,864 - AVERAGE 25,703